CHILDREN'S ENCYCLOPEDIA OF
Dinosaurs

CHILDREN'S ENCYCLOPEDIA OF
Dinosaurs

MICHAEL K. BRETT-SURMAN

WELDON OWEN

Conceived and produced by Weldon Owen Pty Ltd
59–61 Victoria Street, McMahons Point
Sydney NSW 2060, Australia

Copyright © 2010 Weldon Owen Pty Ltd
First published 2008

BONNIER BOOKS
Group Publisher John Owen

WELDON OWEN PTY LTD
Chief Executive Officer Sheena Coupe
Publisher Corinne Roberts
Creative Director Sue Burk
Senior Vice President, International Sales Stuart Laurence
Vice President, Sales: Asia and Latin America Dawn Low
Sales Manager: North America Ellen Towell
Administration Manager, International Sales Kristine Ravn
Production Director Todd Rechner
Production Controller Lisa Conway
Production Coordinator Mike Crowton
Publishing Assistant Nathan Grice

Project Editor Gordana Trifunovic
Editorial Assistant Hunnah Jessup
Designer Michelle Cutler
Cover Design Michelle Cutler
Art Manager Trucie Henderson

ISBN: 978-1-921530-63-0

Colour reproduction by Chroma Graphics (Overseas) Pte Ltd
Printed by Toppan Leefung Printing Ltd
Manufactured in China 5 4 3 2 1

A WELDON OWEN PRODUCTION

Futalongkosaurus

Stegosaurus

Kryptops

Euskelosaurus

Gargoyleosaurus

Albertoceratops

Contents

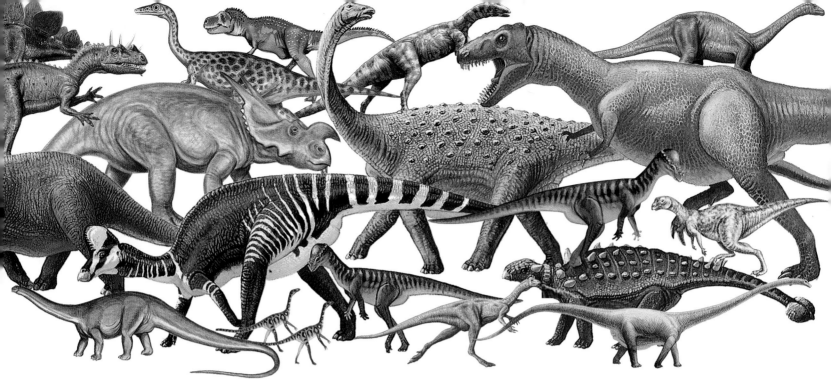

How to use this book

This book is divided into four chapters. The first chapter locates dinosaurs in Earth's history. The second chapter introduces us to dinosaurs and describes what they looked like and how and when they lived. In the third chapter we discover how dinosaurs turn into fossils and how we find and study them. The final chapter is an alphabetical listing of dinosaurs. This is where we describe each dinosaur in detail and where we illustrate each dinosaur.

ABBREVIATIONS

mm	millimeters	t	tonnes
cm	centimeters	kg	kilograms
m	meters	g	grams
km	kilometers	mya	million years ago
sq. km	square kilometers	bya	billion years ago
kph	kilometers per hour		

Chapter name
This shows the name of the chapter.

Introductory text
This text introduces the topic of the page or section.

Did you know? box
This is explained in detail at the bottom of this page.

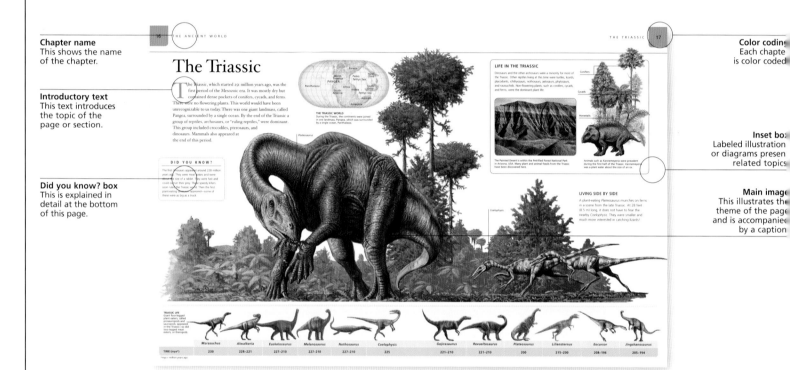

Color coding
Each chapter is color coded

Inset box
Labeled illustration or diagrams present related topics

Main image
This illustrates the theme of the page and is accompanied by a caption

DINOSAUR TIMELINE

A number of spreads in The Ancient World chapter are accompanied by timelines that illustrate the periods in which ancient animals appear.

DID YOU KNOW?

This type of fact box appears on many pages and describes interesting facts about dinosaurs and their environment.

DID YOU KNOW?

Paleontologists learn a lot about extinct animals by studying living ones. For example, the legs of an ostrich are not very different from a meat-eating dinosaur's. By watching ostriches walk, paleontologists can get a good idea of how meat eaters walked.

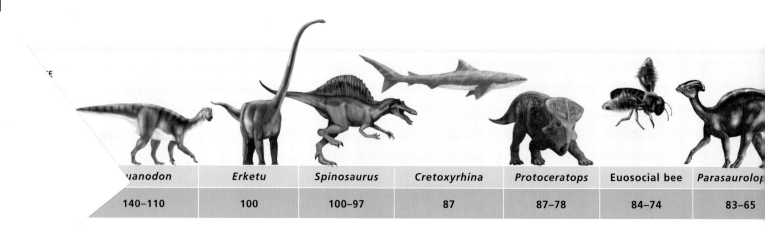

Iguanodon	Erketu	Spinosaurus	Cretoxyrhina	Protoceratops	Euosocial bee	Parasaurolop
140–110	100	100–97	87	87–78	84–74	83–65

Subsections
Within each chapter
are sections, and some
sections have their
own subsections.

Feature box
Interesting aspects
of the topic appear
in feature boxes.

Photo and caption
Captioned photos
show scenes or images
relating to the theme
of the page.

Distribution map
This is explained in
detail at the bottom
of this page.

Dinosaur illustration
Detailed illustrations
show what scientists think
the dinosaur looked like.

The facts
This is explained in
detail at the bottom
of this page.

Running head
The right-hand
running head shows
different sections
within the chapter.

Illustration information
Each illustration is named.
Some illustrations have
additional information.

Full-page feature
Some pages have a
full-page feature.
These show aspects of
the topic in more detail.

Pronunciation guide
This tells you how to
say the dinosaur's name.

Dinosaur profile
This describes the dinosaur
in more detail.

Extra information
Some dinosaurs are featured
on one or two pages and
extra information is given.

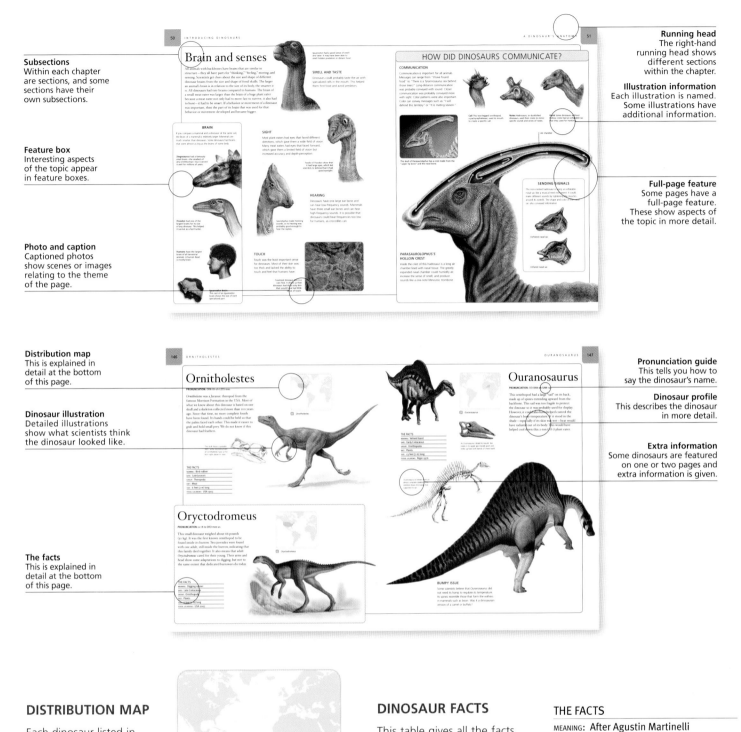

DISTRIBUTION MAP

Each dinosaur listed in
the A–Z of Dinosaurs
chapter is accompanied
by a distribution map. This
shows where the dinosaur
fossils were discovered.

Agustinia

DINOSAUR FACTS

This table gives all the facts
about a dinosaur: what its
name means, when it lived,
what group it is from, what
it ate, how long it was, and
where its fossils were found.

THE FACTS

MEANING: After Agustin Martinelli

DATE: Early Cretaceous

GROUP: Sauropodamorpha

DIET: Herbivorous

SIZE: 50 feet (15 m) long

FOSSIL LOCATIONS: Argentina 1999

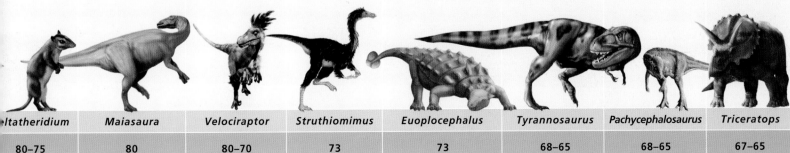

ltatheridium	Maiasaura	Velociraptor	Struthiomimus	Euoplocephalus	Tyrannosaurus	Pachycephalosaurus	Triceratops
80–75	80	80–70	73	73	68–65	68–65	67–65

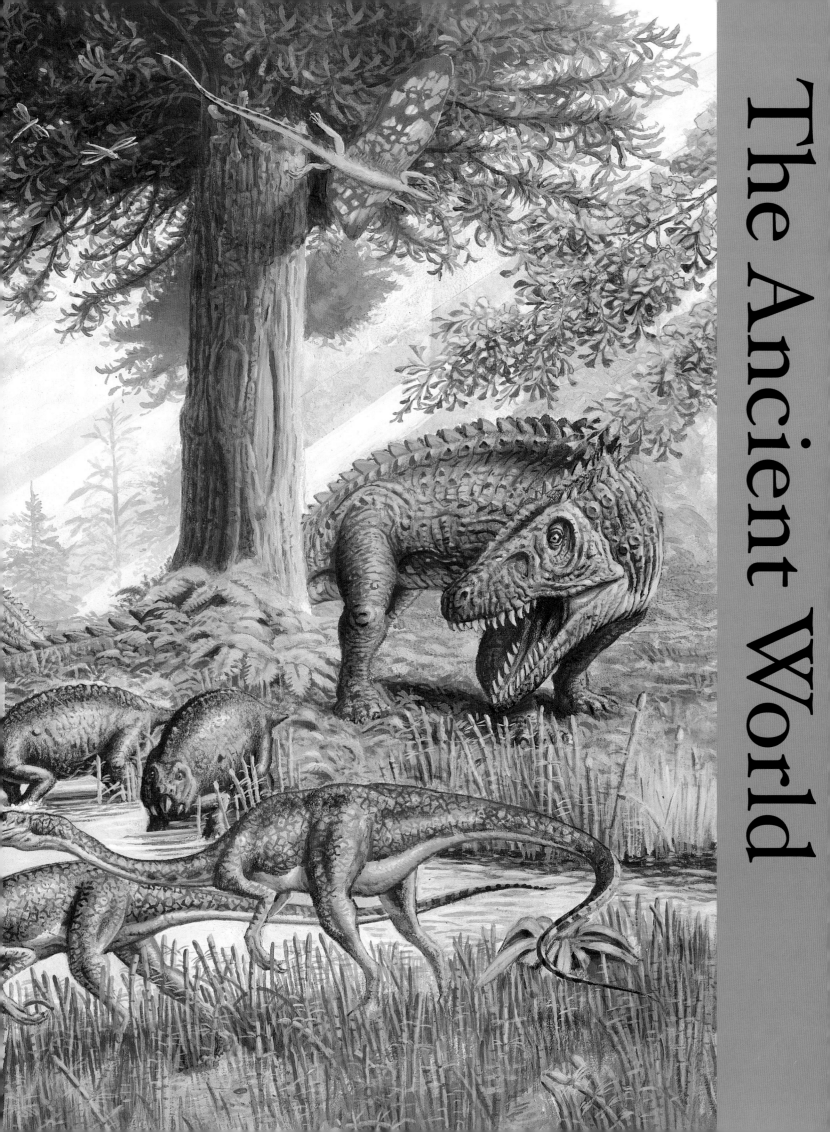

Earth through Time

CONTINENTS IN MOTION

Imagine Earth's crust is broken into pieces—like a jigsaw puzzle. The pieces of the puzzle are called continental plates and, for more than four billion years, these plates have been colliding and moving. The result is that Earth's surface completely changes about every 250 million years. The process, known as "continental drift," is responsible for every major mountain chain, the size and shape of the oceans, and all major earthquakes and volcanoes. The study of continental drift helped answer the early riddle of why scientists have found dicynodonts, small plant-eating animals, on South America, Africa, and Antarctica when these places are separated by oceans. How it this possible? The answer is that, during the Permian period when dicynodonts lived, all these places were one huge supercontinent, called Pangea. This landmass has since split into the separate landmasses of today.

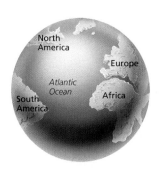

200 million years ago The supercontinent, Pangea, starts to break up into two landmasses, Laurasia in the north and Gondwana in the south, then into smaller ones.

90 million years ago The landmasses break up further—North America, Asia, and Europe in the north, and South America and Africa in the south—see how they look like pieces of a jigsaw?

Present day The Atlantic Ocean is widening and one day it will be as big as the Pacific Ocean. New Hawaiian islands will emerge as the plates pass over volcanic hot spots.

60 million years from now The Mediterranean Sea is starting to disappear, the Alps are getting taller, and the Appalachian Mountains are now just hills.

Scientists believe Earth was formed 4.6 billion years ago. Simple bacteria appeared 3.8 billion years ago but it was not until about 550 million years ago that there was a huge increase in the kinds and numbers of animals—this increase was called the "Cambrian explosion." From this time, Earth's history is divided into three long eras: the Paleozoic, the Age of Ancient Life; the Mesozoic, the Age of Dinosaurs; and the Cenozoic, the Age of Mammals.

WHAT IS A PALEONTOLOGIST?

A paleontologist is a scientist who studies ancient life, especially the fossils of plants and animals. Paleontologists work with geologists, who study Earth, including rocks, minerals, and fossils that give us clues to Earth's history. Both paleontology and geology include the study of geological time, which is the vast length of time that stretches from the formation of Earth to the present day. Geological time is divided into eons, then eras, then periods, epochs, and stages. When paleontologists study dinosaurs, they want to know how dinosaurs interacted with their environment and with other animals, including other dinosaurs.

TIMELINE
This chart shows when many groups of animals first appeared on Earth. Dinosaurs ruled for 160 million years and this, with another 65 million years of bird evolution, is the most successful and diverse land group in Earth's history.

ARCHEAN*	PROTEROZOIC	CAMBRIAN	ORDOVICIAN	SILURIAN	DEVONIAN	CARBONIFEROU
4600–2500 (mya**)	2500–542	542–488	488–444	444–416	416–359	359–299

| PRECAMBRIAN TIME | | | | PALEOZOIC ERA | | |

*Archean and Proterozoic are eons. All the rest are periods.   **mya = million years ago

ROCK RECORDS

THE GRAND CANYON'S ROCK RECORD

Sedimentary rock is formed when rocks are broken up by pounding waves or smashed by other rocks; the tiny pieces settle in layers and, eventually, become sedimentary rock. The study of sedimentary rock tells us what the climate was like when the rock was deposited, and by studying the fossils in the rock, what animals and plants lived at that time. The Grand Canyon is a layer-cake of sedimentary rock formed over millions of years.

The Grand Canyon, in Arizona, USA, is the largest desert canyon in the world. It was slowly carved out by the Colorado River.

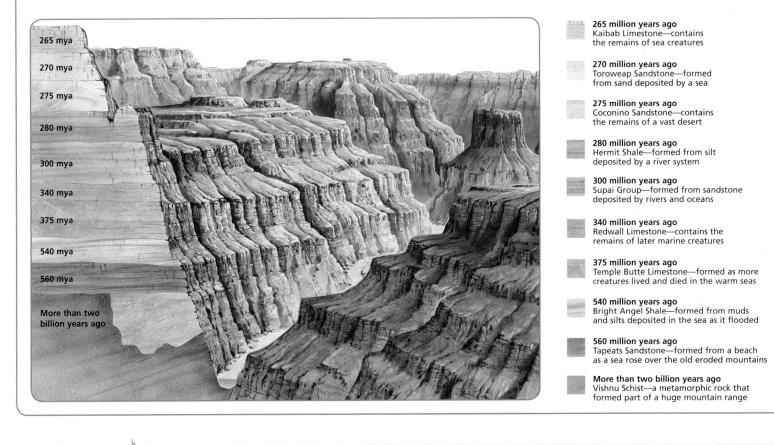

265 mya
270 mya
275 mya
280 mya
300 mya
340 mya
375 mya
540 mya
560 mya

More than two billion years ago

265 million years ago
Kaibab Limestone—contains the remains of sea creatures

270 million years ago
Toroweap Sandstone—formed from sand deposited by a sea

275 million years ago
Coconino Sandstone—contains the remains of a vast desert

280 million years ago
Hermit Shale—formed from silt deposited by a river system

300 million years ago
Supai Group—formed from sandstone deposited by rivers and oceans

340 million years ago
Redwall Limestone—contains the remains of later marine creatures

375 million years ago
Temple Butte Limestone—formed as more creatures lived and died in the warm seas

540 million years ago
Bright Angel Shale—formed from muds and silts deposited in the sea as it flooded

560 million years ago
Tapeats Sandstone—formed from a beach as a sea rose over the old eroded mountains

More than two billion years ago
Vishnu Schist—a metamorphic rock that formed part of a huge mountain range

PERMIAN	TRIASSIC	JURASSIC	CRETACEOUS	PALEOGENE	NEOGENE
299–251	251–200	200–146	146–65.5	65.5–23	23–now
		MESOZOIC ERA		CENOZOIC ERA	

Before the Dinosaurs

Animals with shells
These animals leave much more complete fossils. Trilobite fossils show legs, antennae, and eyes.

Algae and bacteria

Annelids (worms) and arthropods

Jellyfish

Ammonite

Trilobite

Pteraspis

Soft-bodied organisms
Soft-bodied organisms leave fossil records only under rare conditions.

Jawless fish
These armored creatures, such as *Drepanaspis,* used a rasping tongue to gather food from the floor of the shallow seas.

Drepanaspis

Pterygotus

When the first animals walked on land, they had to overcome gravity. The basic design of all animals with backbones changed with the need to carry the body off the ground—and to breathe air. Then they had to lay eggs on land without them drying out. Once reptiles did not need to breed in or near water, they developed into two great groups. One group, the synapsids, eventually led to mammals. The main group, the sauropsids, became reptiles and birds. The beginning of the Triassic was dominated by synapsids but from the end of this period sauropsids, which were better adapted to dry conditions, took over for 140 million years.

Sea scorpions
Active predators such as the sea scorpion, *Pterygotus,* were one of the first groups to venture onto land.

It is rare to find jellyfish fossils. This one was found preserved in sandstone in South Australia.

Ammonites were marine carnivores that died out 65 million years ago. Today they are highly prized fossils.

CARBONIFEROUS COAL

The great forests of the Carboniferous period later formed the vast deposits of coal that fuel today's electricity. The Appalachian mountain range is the main source of coal for the USA.

The *Seymouria* fossil is a key link between amphibians and reptiles.

Trilobites were the most successful marine organism of the early Paleozoic.

Early reptiles
Reptiles such as *Hylonomus* hunted insects. They sheltered inside hollow tree trunks where they were protected from larger reptiles and amphibians.

THE PALEOZOIC WORLD

The Paleozoic era (542–251 million years ago) came before the Mesozoic, the age of dinosaurs. The diverse sea life led to the first land life. Plants arrived; then came the arthropods, fish, amphibians, and, finally, reptiles. At the end of the Paleozoic era, the greatest extinction event in Earth's history made it possible for reptiles to take over.

Dunkleosteus
This placoderm could pierce the armor of other armored fish.

Amphibians
These animals had fin-limbs that allowed them to walk onto land in search of food.

Insects
They were the first animals to have true (powered) flight. *Meganeura*, a dragonfly, had a 3-foot (1-m) wingspan.

Synapsids
Synapsids were the top predators of the Permian. This *Dimetrodon* had a distinctive "sail" on its back.

Pseudosuchians
Pseudosuchians were the ancestors of dinosaurs and crocodiles. They dominated the early Triassic.

The Triassic

The Triassic, which started 251 million years ago, was the first period of the Mesozoic era. It was mostly dry but contained dense pockets of conifers, cycads, and ferns. There were no flowering plants. This world would have been unrecognizable to us today. There was one giant landmass, called Pangea, surrounded by a single ocean. By the end of the Triassic a group of reptiles, archosaurs, or "ruling reptiles," were dominant. This group included crocodiles, pterosaurs, and dinosaurs. Mammals also appeared at the end of this period.

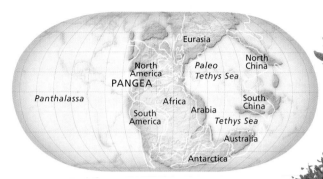

THE TRIASSIC WORLD
During the Triassic, the continents were joined in one landmass, Pangea, which was surrounded by a single ocean, Panthalassa.

DID YOU KNOW?

The first dinosaurs appeared around 228 million years ago. They were meat eaters and were about the size of a rabbit. They were fast and could outrun their prey. These speedy killers soon ruled the Triassic world. Then the first plant-eating dinosaurs appeared—some of these were as big as a truck.

Plateosaurus

TRIASSIC LIFE
Giant four-legged plant eaters, called prosauropods and sauropods, appeared in the Triassic—so did two-legged meat eaters, or theropods.

TIME (mya*)	Marasuchus	Alwalkeria	Euskelosaurus	Melanosaurus	Nothosaurus	Coelophysis
	230	228–221	227–210	227–210	227–210	225

*mya = million years ago

LIFE IN THE TRIASSIC

Dinosaurs and the other archosaurs were a minority for most of the Triassic. Other reptiles living at this time were turtles, lizards, placodonts, ichthyosaurs, nothosaurs, aetosaurs, phytosaurs, and rauisuchids. Non-flowering plants, such as conifers, cycads, and ferns, were the dominant plant life.

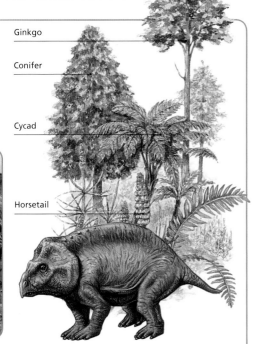

Ginkgo

Conifer

Cycad

Horsetail

The Painted Desert is within the Petrified Forest National Park in Arizona, USA. Many plant and animal fossils from the Triassic have been discovered here.

Animals such as *Kannemeyeria* were prevalent during the first half of the Triassic. *Kannemeyeria* was a plant eater about the size of an ox.

LIVING SIDE BY SIDE

A plant-eating *Plateosaurus* munches on ferns in a scene from the late Triassic. At 28 feet (8.5 m) long, it does not have to fear the nearby *Coelophysis*. They were smaller and much more interested in catching lizards!

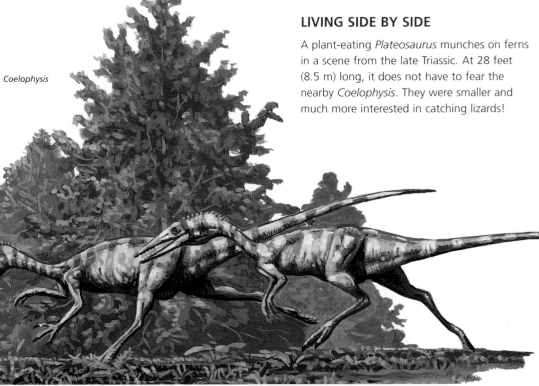

Coelophysis

Gojirasaurus	Revueltosaurus	Plateosaurus	Liliensternus	Eocursor	Jingshanosaurus
221–210	221–210	200	215–200	208–196	205–194

The Jurassic

Pangea was starting to break apart into Gondwana in the southern hemisphere and Laurasia in the northern hemisphere. The world was wet and warm. There was no grass and no flowers, and forests grew thick with conifers, cycads, and ferns. Dinosaurs began to flourish, especially the saurischians, or the "lizard-hipped" dinosaurs, which included sauropods and theropods. Sauropods were huge plant eaters and they feasted on treetops. Some sauropods, if living today, would be able to look in the window of a five-story building. Theropods were the fastest animals on Earth and they ate meat—dinosaurs and other reptiles served as their expanding food source. Feathers developed during the Jurassic.

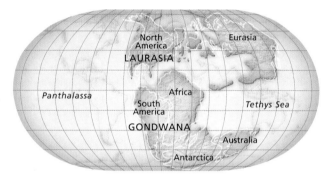

THE JURASSIC WORLD
North America drifted away from Eurasia and Africa, opening up the ancient Atlantic. In the south, the landmass Gondwana remained largely intact.

Allosaur

FIGHT FOR SURVIVAL

Diplodocus, a sauropod, rears up to scare off three allosaurs, which were meat eaters. The adult *Diplodocus* is too big to be killed outright but the young one beside it is just the right size. Can the quicker allosaurs get past the whip-tail of *Diplodocus*? Fossils in Wyoming, USA, show that if *Diplodocus* came crashing down on any part of an allosaur, it would squash it flat. Any major injury could be fatal.

JURASSIC LIFE
Jurassic conditions were just right for dinosaurs and many new types appeared by the end of the Jurassic period. They were living all over the two continents.

	Megazostrodon	*Limulidae*	*Scelidosaurus*	*Dilophosaurus*	*Shunosaurus*	*Guanlong*	*Liopleuroc*
TIME (mya*)	more than 200	200–144	202–195	202–190	169–159	160	160–155

*mya = million years ago

Diplodocus

LIFE IN THE JURASSIC

The Jurassic landscape was not as dry as the Triassic one. The warm and humid climate produced larger and thicker forests.

Conifers

Cycads

Ferns

At Stair Hole, in Dorset, England, you can see where the sea has eroded the hard Jurassic rock in the cliff face.

There was plenty of dinosaur food in the Jurassic world. Meat eaters feasted on turtles, crocodiles, lizards, and insects.

Young Diplodocus

uojiangosaurus	Archeopteryx	Sinraptor	Brachiosaurus	Mamenchisaurus	Diplodocus	Stegosaurus	Brachytrachelopan
156	156–150	154–150	153–113	151–144	150	150	150

The Cretaceous

The Cretaceous lasted 80 million years. It began when conifers and cycads were the dominant plants and ended with flowering plants being more common. The flower was a new source of food for plant eaters. The continents split and dinosaurs could evolve in isolation. Tyrannosaurs were the ruling meat-eating dinosaurs in the northern hemisphere, and abelisaurs in the southern hemisphere. By the end of the Cretaceous, all the dinosaurs had died out, except birds.

THE CRETACEOUS WORLD
During this time the southern landmass of Gondwana broke into separate landmasses. The weather became more seasonal. Summer was warm and wet and winter got chilly.

Pterosaur

Styracosaurus

Troodon

Tyrannosaurus

Parasaurolophus

Nodrosaurus

CRETACEOUS LIFE
Modern groups began to take over every major environment in the Cretaceous period—on land, sea, and air.

	Iguanodon	Erketu	Spinosaurus	Cretoxyrhina	Protoceratops	Euosocial bee	Parasaurolop
TIME (mya*)	146–110	100	100–97	87	87–78	84–74	83–65

*mya = million years ago

LIFE IN THE CRETACEOUS

The biggest change in this period was the appearance of flowering plants. By the end of the Cretaceous, there were many different types, such as water lilies, magnolias, and sycamores. This new food source resulted in more types of dinosaurs than ever before.

Conifer

Water lilies

Magnolias

Insects such as bees relied on flowering plants for food and the plants relied on the bees for pollination.

The Seven Sisters Cliffs, in East Essex, England, are typical of the white chalk cliffs that were formed during the Cretaceous period.

Carnotaurus

CRETACEOUS DINOSAURS

This scene shows a variety of Cretaceous dinosaurs from all areas. Theropods such as *Carnotaurus* watch as abelisaurs approach from the left. In the background, a herd of *Parasaurolophus*, which are hadrosaurs, or duckbilled dinosaurs, leave the area. Above them are flying reptiles, or pterosaurs. In the foreground is an armored *Nodosaur*, which is an ankylosaur.

tatheridium	Maiasaura	Velociraptor	Struthiomimus	Euoplocephalus	Tyrannosaurus	Pachycephalosaurus	Triceratops
80–75	80	80–70	73	73	68–65	68–65	67–65

The Early Reptiles

Reptiles were around for 100 million years before the first dinosaur appeared on Earth. Their biggest evolutionary achievement was the amniotic egg. An amniotic egg has its own food supply and its own waste chamber, and it can be laid on land. This allowed reptiles to branch out onto all land—not just land that was near water. The other group of land animals were the synapsids, the ancestors of mammals, but they needed much more water for survival. Reptiles could exist and evolve in many more environments than synapsids could—this is an important reason why reptiles dominated Earth for more than 200 million years.

Permian gliding reptile

Carboniferous ancestral reptile

Mesozoic turtle

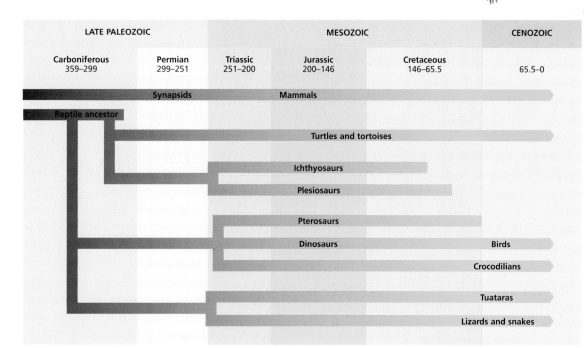

LATE PALEOZOIC			MESOZOIC		CENOZOIC
Carboniferous 359–299	Permian 299–251	Triassic 251–200	Jurassic 200–146	Cretaceous 146–65.5	65.5–0

Synapsids — Mammals

Reptile ancestor

Turtles and tortoises

Ichthyosaurs

Plesiosaurs

Pterosaurs

Dinosaurs — Birds

Crocodilians

Tuataras

Lizards and snakes

REPTILE TIMELINE

This chart shows how some of the main groups of reptiles are related. One of the first known true reptiles was *Petrolacosaurus* in the Carboniferous period.

SYNAPSIDS

Once known incorrectly as "mammal-like reptiles," synapsids were not reptiles but the main competition for true reptiles. They were the dominant meat eaters of the Permian before reptiles took over during the Triassic. Synapsids may also have been the first group of animals to develop body hair.

Cynognathus is close to the first mammal. It has the same kinds of teeth that we have: incisors, canines, premolars, and molars.

DIFFERENT EGGS

The reptile egg (left) is like a suitcase with its own food supply. An amphibian egg (below) needs to be laid in water.

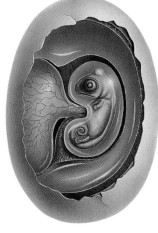

Reptile egg

Amphibian egg

Flying Cretaceous pterosaur

Jurassic dinosaur *Stegosaurus*

Cenozoic snake

Triassic lizard

Mesozoic crocodile

Cretaceous sea turtle

A GALLERY OF REPTILES FROM ACROSS TIME

Not all reptiles lived at the same time, and in the same place. Like today, many animals lived only in certain areas, and in certain climates. *Stegosaurus* in the Jurassic never saw the flying *Pteranodon* in the Cretaceous.

Small Mesozoic ichthyosaur

Long-necked Jurassic plesiosaur

Cretaceous sea turtle

Reptiles of the air and sea

There were more than 40 major groups of reptiles in the Mesozoic era and dinosaurs made up only two of those groups. The other non-dinosaur reptiles lived in lakes, seas, and the air. The pterosaurs had two subgroups, the Rhamphorhyncoids, mostly Triassic and Jurassic, and the Pterodactyloids, mostly Cretaceous. The largest flying animal of all time was the azhdarchid pterodactyl, with a wingspan of more than 49 feet (15 m). Ichthyosaurs, which looked like dolphins, were abundant during the first half of the Mesozoic.

IN THE SKIES

These three Rhamphorhyncoids represent the first wave of vertebrates to have true flight—powered flight that does not rely on gliding or parachuting. They were usually smaller than 13 feet (4 m) across and ate insects and animals small enough to be swallowed whole.

Scaphognathus

Dimorphodon

Rhamphorhynchus

An example of a limb fossil from a plesiosaur. They used their limbs like paddles to propel through the water.

A pterodactyl fossil clearly showing that, unlike bats, pterodactyl wings were supported only by the fourth finger.

Pachypleurosaurs, plesiosaurs, ranged in size from 8 inches to 3 feet (20 cm–1 m).

IN THE OCEANS

Marine reptiles were the top predators in the Mesozoic seas. Today their job is held by sharks and marine mammals. Some reptiles, such as ichthyosaurs, used their tails for propulsion, while others, such as pliosaurs, used "paddle-power." Long-neck reptiles were ambush predators while short-necks were high-speed pursuit predators.

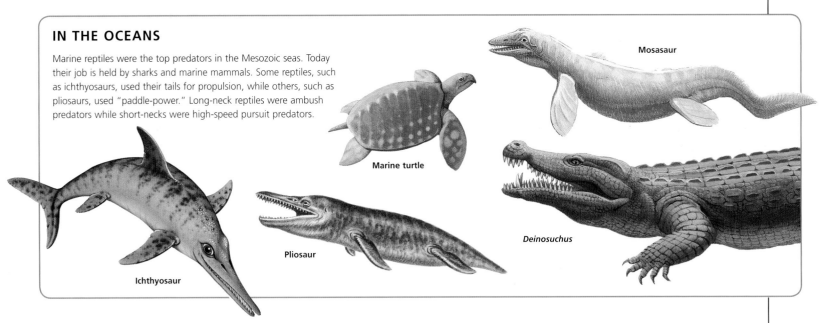

Mosasaur

Marine turtle

Deinosuchus

Pliosaur

Ichthyosaur

ON THE HUNT FOR FOOD

This pterosaur, *Rhamphorhynchus,* is flying over a plesiosaur attacking a school of fish. It hopes to catch some wounded fish or fish at the surface trying to escape the plesiosaur. *Rhamphorhynchus* is far too small to challenge marine reptiles. Notice how its teeth point forward for spearing fish.

Dinosaurs, Feathers, and Flight

FIRST FLIGHT

Archeopteryx flies after a dragonfly in a Jurassic forest of Germany. This "first bird" is known from only ten fossil specimens.

Less than one generation ago, scientists thought birds were the only animals ever to have had feathers. We now know that more than five groups of non-bird theropods had feathers. The first downy feathers were for temperature control. Next were body and contour feathers and, finally, ornamental feathers. We also thought birds were the only ones to have their collarbones fused together to form wishbones, to have a half-moon-shaped wristbone, and to have a pubic bone that pointed backward—we now know that non-bird theropods also had them. The first theropod with true flight was *Archeopteryx*, from the late Jurassic.

An *Archeopteryx* feather fossil.

Caudipteryx from the Chinese Cretaceous had feathers but it was too small for true flight.

FROM ARM TO WING

Through time, dinosaurs' arms evolved into wings. The mass of the bulky flight muscles moved from the upper arm to the breastbone to lighten the arm. The arm bones got longer to provide more room for feathers to attach. The wristbones moved in only one direction, which limited movement but gave extra stability.

Sinosauropteryx stage
The short, stubby arms were feathered, but unsuitable for flight.

Caudipteryx stage
The forearm doubled in length and there were longer feathers.

Microraptor stage
The arm and feathers are ready but the muscles are too weak.

Confuciusornis stage
All forearm and flight muscles are developed enough for true flight.

EVOLUTION OF BIRDS

MODERN BIRDS

Mesozoic theropods, which were not birds, had many but not all of the features of birds. Birds range in size from today's tiny 2¼-inch (5.5-cm) Cuban Bee Hummingbird to the non-flying Cretaceous "terror-birds," such as the meat-eating flightless phorusrhacid from South America that was 10 feet (3 m) tall—or the huge bird of prey, the flying teratorn, that had a 19-foot (6-m) wingspan.

SNOW GOOSE
This bird can master flight in many conditions.

DINOSAUR TO BIRD

For stable flight, the "center of mass" lies close to the "center of power." The pelvis and sternum are on top of each other and the sternum is much bigger, the arms longer, the bones more hollow, and the tail shorter but wider.

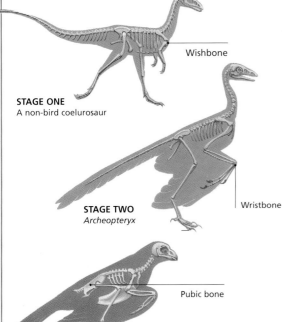

Wishbone

STAGE ONE
A non-bird coelurosaur

STAGE TWO
Archeopteryx

Wristbone

Pubic bone

STAGE THREE
Pigeon

ICHTHYORNIS
It had teeth, unlike birds today, and flew over Cretaceous seas.

FOSSIL RECORD

The change from theropod to bird is one of the best documented transitions in the fossil record.

ARCHEOPTERYX
Flight feathers were present but it was a weak flyer.

Wing bone

FLIGHT MUSCLES
There are two sets of flight muscles, one for the power stroke and one for the recovery stroke.

Flight muscle (pectoris)

Breastbone (keeled sternum)

THEROPOD
The long arms and air-sac system were already present.

Dinosaur Extinction

A mass extinction occurs when most life on Earth is destroyed. There have been five "mass extinctions" during Earth's history. The extinction event at the end of the Mesozoic era wiped out 66 percent of life. Most were species that lived on land and larger species were affected more than small ones.

We know that the extinction happened about 65.5 million years ago, but there is a range of error and variation of 500,000 years. Scientists believe that an asteroid hit Earth but do not know if it was one asteroid, or a big one plus smaller ones that hit before and after the big one. An asteroid is a small rocky body that circles the Sun.

FIGHT FOR SURVIVAL

Dinosaurs that lived within a 600-mile (1,000-km) radius of the impact would have been killed directly. Did it take many thousands of years for the entire world's ecosystems to collapse beyond recovery? Why did the ecologically fragile frogs survive but not primitive birds that lived worldwide and could fly away?

A CLIMATE TIMELINE
Earth has gone from a hothouse to a freezer box many times during its long history. The more gradual the change, the better life can adapt.

3.7 bya Climate 18°F (10°C) warmer than today

330 mya Start of long ice age

2.7–1.8 bya
Ice sheets widespread

450 mya
Brief ice age

245 mya
Climate warms, dinosaurs appear

Present average temperature

bya = billion years ago   mya = million years ago   ya = years ago

ASTEROID IMPACT

Many asteroids have hit Earth but few are associated with major extinction events. The Chicxulub asteroid hit during an age of intense, continental-size volcanic activity. This asteroid is estimated to have been 7,500 feet (12,000 m) in diameter. The impact would have set off magnitude-10 earthquakes and supergiant tsunamis, and created an ash cloud that would have covered the whole of Earth's atmosphere. It is possible that the asteroid, together with the volcanic activity, could have started a series of chain reactions that eventually caused the extinctions.

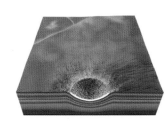
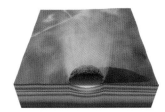

1. Ball of fire
The asteroid becomes a ball of fire and by the time it strikes Earth's surface it is white hot.

2. On impact
The impact sends a cloud of vaporized rock into the air. Some of this material may go into orbit around Earth.

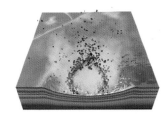
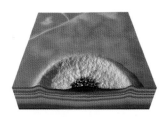

3. Mineral fragments
As the vapor cools it condenses into minerals that fall over a wide area. Heated rocks below ground explode.

4. Crater impact
The crater is circular, regardless of the angle of the strike. Most craters have a central mound and a raised rim.

Wolfe Creek Crater, in Western Australia, was created when a meteorite crashed to Earth 300,000 years ago. This crater is internationally significant as one of only 18 craters in the world where fragments of meteorite remain on the site.

OTHER EXTINCTION THEORIES

There have been more than 40 extinction theories, such as widespread poisoning and disease. Many are now considered to be comical, such as the theory that the rise of flowering plants caused dinosaurs to develop terminal allergies to pollen.

Other outlandish theories include the claims that dinosaurs died of boredom, drowned in their own dung, or were not intelligent enough to survive. We know that none of these is true—there is no evidence to support them.

Poles apart Overheating of the atmosphere could explain some extinctions, but not the disappearance of dinosaurs that lived close to the poles.

Ice age There was no ice age at the end of the Cretaceous. This era was warmer than any world climate has been in the past four million years.

Volcanoes Volcanic eruptions cause extinctions only when they erupt over areas the size of countries and erupt for many thousands of years.

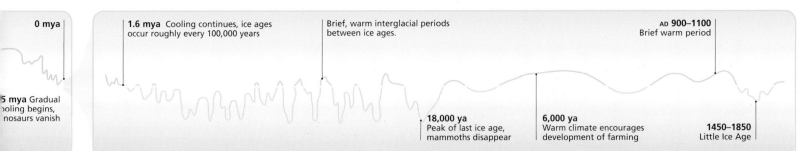

0 mya

1.6 mya Cooling continues, ice ages occur roughly every 100,000 years

Brief, warm interglacial periods between ice ages.

AD **900–1100** Brief warm period

5 mya Gradual cooling begins, dinosaurs vanish

18,000 ya Peak of last ice age, mammoths disappear

6,000 ya Warm climate encourages development of farming

1450–1850 Little Ice Age

After the dinosaurs

Immediately after the mass extinction event, at the beginning of the Paleogene period, most large land-living animals had died off. With the extinction of many of their predators, surviving mammals evolved into thousands of different species and replaced dinosaurs as the ruling animals on Earth. Some birds, such as *Phorusrhacos*, came to be as large as Jurassic meat eaters, or theropods. Famous predators, such as the cave bear, saber-toothed tiger, and the dire wolf, appeared less than a million years ago. They missed the Mesozoic era by 64 million years.

VICTIMS AND SURVIVORS

Smaller animals did better than larger ones during the extinction event. It took another 15 million years after the event for animals on Earth to become as big as dinosaurs were.

VICTIMS	EXTINCTION EVENT	SURVIVORS
Non-avian dinosaurs		
Pterosaurs		
Ichthyosaurs		
Mosasaurs		
Plesiosaurs		
Ammonites		
Mammals		
Birds		
Snakes		
Lizards		
Crocodiles		
Turtles		
Gharials		

Phorusrhacos, the "terror-bird," was more than 7 feet (2.2 m) tall.

The gomphothere elephant of the Paleogene period had "shovel-tusks" in its lower jaw.

Small mammals such as this *Purgatorius* survived the mass extinction.

The saber-toothed tiger had teeth designed for stabbing, which made it a fierce predator. It became extinct shortly after human contact.

THE FIRST HUMANS

This skull of a *Homo erectus* shows the thick brow over the eyes. It was this species that first reached modern size in body and brain.

There have been many species of *Homo*, the group that humans belong to. Human evolution took place in the last few million years. Anthropology is the science of humanity's past and present, its culture, and the physical changes in the body. The first humans lived in a savanna, or grassland, environment as hunter–gatherers. Their bodies did not possess the weapons that dinosaurs had, so humans eventually invented tools to supplement their needs.

There are many species that use tools. However, only humans can take natural objects and make them into new objects—and combine them into more tools.

This saber-toothed tiger is stuck in a Pleistocene tar pit (about 12,000 years ago). Hundreds of skeletons have been found at the La Brea Tar Pit in California, USA.

SURVIVING RELATIVES

DIRECT DESCENDANTS

The "ruling reptiles," the archosaurs, have representatives living today. The crocodiles persist as a few species out of more than a hundred species in the Mesozoic era. Of the seven major groups of dinosaurs, only the theropods still have direct descendants living today—the birds. They are now the most numerous of all land vertebrates, even though they are restricted to smaller sizes compared to mammals. They live on every continent, including the antarctic, and in every environment. They can migrate farther than any mammal, and they can fly higher.

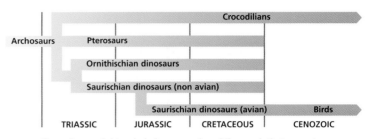

Archosaurs					Crocodilians		
	Pterosaurs						
	Ornithischian dinosaurs						
	Saurischian dinosaurs (non avian)						
			Saurischian dinosaurs (avian)			Birds	
TRIASSIC		JURASSIC		CRETACEOUS		CENOZOIC	

Non-avian saurischians include sauropods and theropods that are not on the line to birds. Avian saurischians include deinonychosaurs and birds.

Living crocodiles have a bite force that is comparable to that of the mighty tyrannosaurs. They can also bite faster than the eye can see. Never underestimate a "ruling reptile!"

DISTANT COUSINS

Crocodiles and their relatives lived in more Mesozoic environments than the dinosaurs, including the sea. Then there were many species but today they are restricted to just three groups—crocodiles, alligators, and gharials.

Like *Archeopteryx*, the modern-day Hoatzin nestling has three claws on the end of each wing. They drop when the bird grows older.

POWERED FLIGHT

Flying theropods, which are today known as birds, have perfected powered flight. They can live in all environments and can migrate from pole to pole. However, does this make them extinction-proof?

Introducing Dinosaurs

What is a Dinosaur?

There are about 800 different kinds of dinosaurs— and one new dinosaur is recorded every two weeks. The word *dinosaur* means "a fearfully great, or terrible, lizard," but this does not apply to all dinosaurs. Some dinosaurs were bigger than a bus while others were as small as a chicken. Although there were different kinds of dinosaurs they had many things in common. They all walked with their legs directly under their bodies and they were the only reptiles ever to do this. They laid eggs, and most had scaly skin although some may have had feathers.

HATCHED FROM AN EGG
All dinosaurs came out of an egg. All their famous features, such as armor, spikes, and horns, grew just before they became adults.

Fused bones
The hip bone was fused to the backbone for extra strength and weight bearing. Together these bones are called the sacrum.

Allosaurus

Stegosaurus

Camptosaurus

Tyrannosaurus

Coelurus

Corythosaurus

Saltasaurus

Pachycephalosaurus

Triceratops

Euoplocephalus

Hip bones
The hip bone supports the muscles that grip the thighbone tightly. Other muscles move the legs backward and forward.

ANCESTORS IN COMMON
Dinosaurs came in all sizes, shapes, and colors. They came with and without armor, horns, beaks, and claws, yet they were all classified with the first two dinosaurs to be scientifically named—*Iguanodon* and *Megalosaurus*.

Head
Some dinosaurs had strange headgear. This crest was used either to attract a mate or to ward off rivals.

Upright stance
Legs directly under the body allowed for a longer stride, which made dinosaurs faster than reptiles with a sprawling stance. The longer the legs, the longer the stride.

Longest finger
The longest finger in the hand, especially in theropods, was designed to grasp. Other reptiles cannot do this.

DILOPHOSAURUS

This Triassic theropod was typical of early two-legged dinosaurs. The arms no longer supported weight as in four-legged dinosaurs, but were adapted for hunting. The center of mass had moved back toward the pelvis, which made balancing on two legs easier.

WHAT IS NOT A DINOSAUR?

During the Mesozoic era there were up to 40 groups of reptiles but only two were dinosaurs. Dinosaurs did not live in the sea but some of their distant relatives ruled the ancient seas. With the exception of pterosaurs, almost all the other groups had a sprawling stance. Early dinosaurs could not fly either—pterosaurs, or flying reptiles, did that.

PTEROSAURS
Pterosaurs were cousins of dinosaurs. They were divided into two groups—rhamphorhynchoids (dominant in the Jurassic) and pterodactyls (dominant in the Cretaceous).

Scaphognathus

NOTHOSAURS
Ocean-dwelling reptiles, whose name means "false lizard", were similar to the later plesiosaurs but thrived during the Triassic.

Nothosaurus

PELYCOSAURS
These synapsids, once called "mammal-like reptiles," were genetically closer to mammals than reptiles. *Dimetrodon* lived 75 million years before the dinosaurs.

Dimetrodon

PLIOSAURS
This group of marine predators had a short neck and an elongated head, unlike their relatives, the long necked plesiosaurs.

Liopleurodon

CROCODILES
Although there are few species today, there used to be dozens. Some lived only on land and others only in the sea. *Bernissartia* was the smallest at only 2 feet (60 cm) long.

Bernissartia

Different Dinosaurs

There were many kinds of dinosaurs—including some of the largest and longest animals ever to have lived. During their 165 million years on Earth, different groups of dinosaurs adjusted to many surroundings. They lived in all areas and in all climates. They also had to adapt to other animals, including other dinosaurs that competed with them for food and shelter.

This is why there were so many kinds of dinosaurs. There were two-legged meat eaters; long-necked, four-legged plant eaters; two-legged plant eaters; two-legged plant-eaters with duckbills; four-legged, horned plant eaters with short tails; and four-legged, armored plant eaters—and more!

DUCKBILL DINOSAURS

Duckbill dinosaurs used their beaks to cut off leaves and stalks for eating. They also had hundreds of teeth at the back of their mouths that they used to grind up food before they swallowed it. They had four jaws, each with three rows of about 60 teeth—a total of 720. These were replaced as they wore away, so they had thousands of teeth in a lifetime.

Duckbill dinosaurs' beaks were covered in bone and were sharp enough to cut through most plants.

Lambeosaurus This duckbill dinosaur made hornlike sounds with a hollow crest on top of its head. This was a good way to communicate with its herd.

DID YOU KNOW?

There is no such thing as a typical dinosaur, just as there is no such thing as a typical mammal. For every dinosaur you might think is a good standard dinosaur, there is another that is different. There are too many different types of dinosaurs to work out an "average" size, length, or weight.

STEGOSAUR

Stegosaurus had a small head compared to the rest of its body. It was a four-legged, armored plant eater.

CERATOPSIAN

Albertoceratops had horns and spikes on its head but not on its body. It was a four-legged plant eater with a short tail.

LONG-NECKED SAUROPOD

Futalongkosaurus was a long-necked, four-legged plant eater. It was one of the largest animals to ever have lived. It grew to 110 feet (33 m) long.

Dilong Theropods were the first animals to stand on two legs and the first to have feathers. *Dilong* had body feathers but could not fly.

THEROPODS

All theropods were two-legged meat eaters. Most were lightly built with large heads. They usually had bladelike serrated teeth, or teeth with sawlike edges, which they used to tear up their food before they swallowed it.

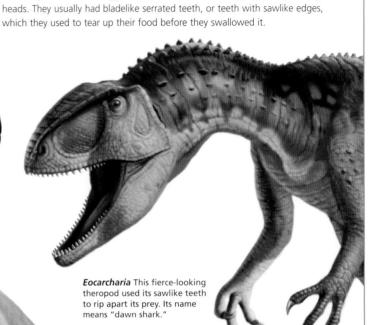

Eocarcharia This fierce-looking theropod used its sawlike teeth to rip apart its prey. Its name means "dawn shark."

PACHYCEPHALOSAUR

Dracorex had horns and bumps on its head. It was a two-legged plant eater. Pachycephalosaur means "thick-headed lizard."

ANKYLOSAUR

Gargoyleosaurus was one of the smallest ankylosaurs, or four-legged, armored plant eaters. It was only 10 feet (3 m) long.

Different hip bones

Dinosaurs are divided into two major groups, the saurischian ("lizard-hipped") dinosaurs and the ornithischian ("bird-hipped") dinosaurs. What we call the hip, or the pelvis, has three bones—the pubis, ilium, and ischium. All dinosaurs had the same three bones but in two different patterns. The pubis had muscles that attached to ribs—this helped breathing and gave gut support. The pubis pointed forward and down in saurischians and backward in the plant-eating ornithischians. The ischium had muscles that moved the legs and tail. In ornithischians, the pubis acted more as an aid to breathing than as gut support.

> **DID YOU KNOW?**
>
> Even though ornithischians are "bird-hipped," birds evolved from saurischians, or "lizard-hipped" dinosaurs. Ornithsichians died out long ago but saurischians live on as birds. All hips—even humans'—are made from the same three bones but in different patterns.

Ilium
Supported the leg muscles.
It transferred leg movement
to the rest of the body.

Ischium
Pointed backward.
It supported muscles
that carried the tail
off the ground.

Pubis
Pointed forward in
saurischians. It helped
support strong gut muscles.

SAURISCHIAN DINOSAURS

Allosaurus was a saurischian. Note the hole in the middle of the pelvis. This is where the thighbone of both saurischians and ornithischians inserted itself. The "rocker" at the end of the pubis was designed to take the weight of this predatory theropod when it lowered itself to the ground to rest.

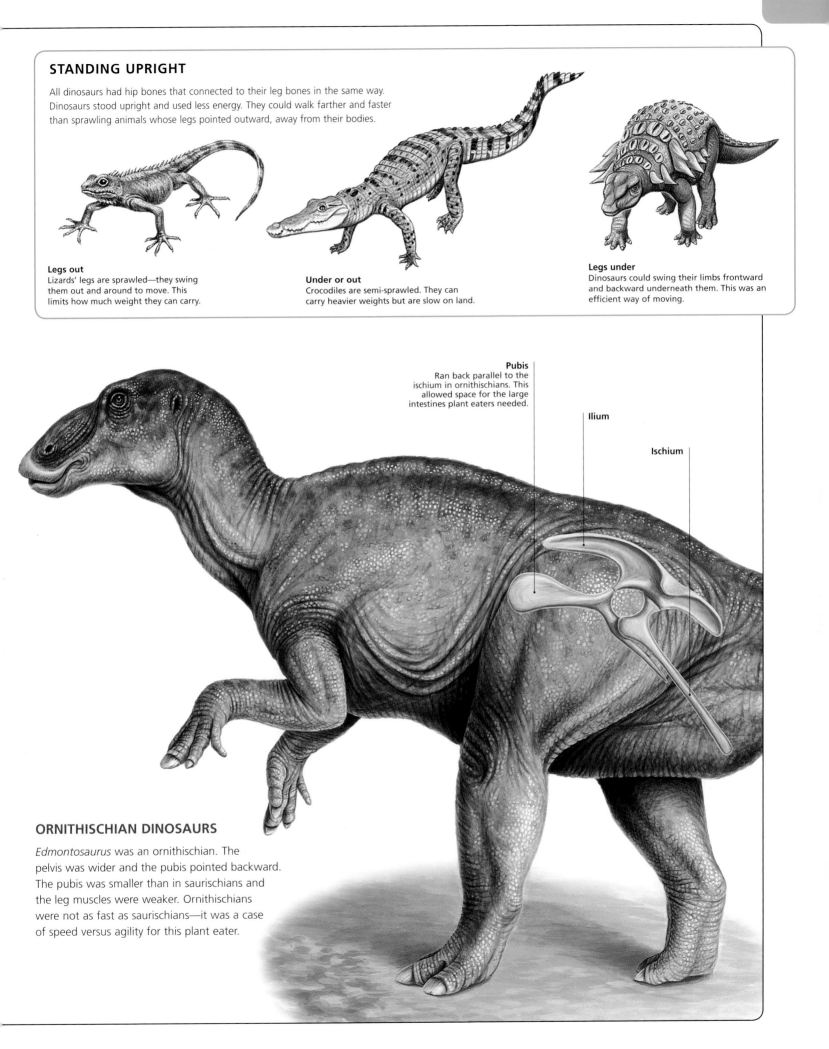

STANDING UPRIGHT

All dinosaurs had hip bones that connected to their leg bones in the same way. Dinosaurs stood upright and used less energy. They could walk farther and faster than sprawling animals whose legs pointed outward, away from their bodies.

Legs out
Lizards' legs are sprawled—they swing them out and around to move. This limits how much weight they can carry.

Under or out
Crocodiles are semi-sprawled. They can carry heavier weights but are slow on land.

Legs under
Dinosaurs could swing their limbs frontward and backward underneath them. This was an efficient way of moving.

Pubis
Ran back parallel to the ischium in ornithischians. This allowed space for the large intestines plant eaters needed.

Ilium

Ischium

ORNITHISCHIAN DINOSAURS

Edmontosaurus was an ornithischian. The pelvis was wider and the pubis pointed backward. The pubis was smaller than in saurischians and the leg muscles were weaker. Ornithischians were not as fast as saurischians—it was a case of speed versus agility for this plant eater.

DINOSAUR GROUPS

Dinosaurs were all archosaurs ("ruling repltiles"). They were either saurischians, which were the dominant dinosaurs in the Triassic and Jurassic, or ornithischians, which were dominant in the Cretaceous. Saurischians are further divided into theropods and sauropods. Theropods were meat eaters such as *Tyrannosaurus rex* and *Deinonychus*—and eventually birds. Sauropods were long-necked plant eaters such as *Diplodocus*. The second major group, the ornithischians, were all plant eaters. Ornithischians are further divided into the armored and plated thyreophorans, and the cerapods. Cerapods include the two-legged dome-heads and the horned dinosaurs such as *Triceratops*.

SAURISCHIANS ("lizard hipped")

THEROPODS

Theropods were the first dinosaurs to appear and were the most successful of all dinosaurs. They were the first land animals to have a fully upright stance and the first animals to have feathers. Theropods include all meat-eating dinosaurs.

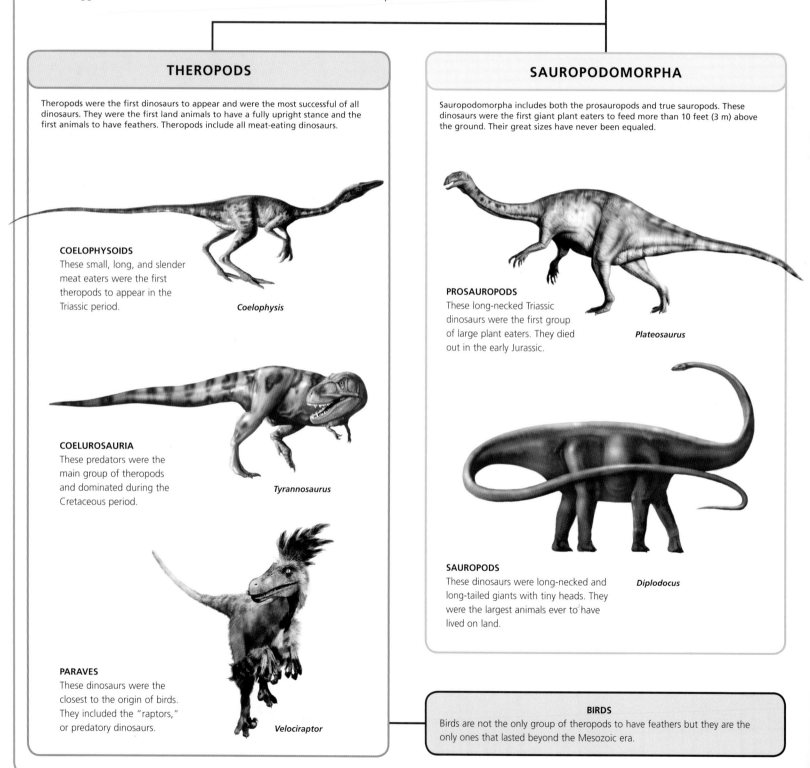

COELOPHYSOIDS
These small, long, and slender meat eaters were the first theropods to appear in the Triassic period.

Coelophysis

COELUROSAURIA
These predators were the main group of theropods and dominated during the Cretaceous period.

Tyrannosaurus

PARAVES
These dinosaurs were the closest to the origin of birds. They included the "raptors," or predatory dinosaurs.

Velociraptor

SAUROPODOMORPHA

Sauropodomorpha includes both the prosauropods and true sauropods. These dinosaurs were the first giant plant eaters to feed more than 10 feet (3 m) above the ground. Their great sizes have never been equaled.

PROSAUROPODS
These long-necked Triassic dinosaurs were the first group of large plant eaters. They died out in the early Jurassic.

Plateosaurus

SAUROPODS
These dinosaurs were long-necked and long-tailed giants with tiny heads. They were the largest animals ever to have lived on land.

Diplodocus

BIRDS
Birds are not the only group of theropods to have feathers but they are the only ones that lasted beyond the Mesozoic era.

ARCHOSAURS ("ruling reptiles") dinosaurs, pterosaurs, pseudosuchians, and crocodiles

ORNITHISCHIANS ("bird hipped")

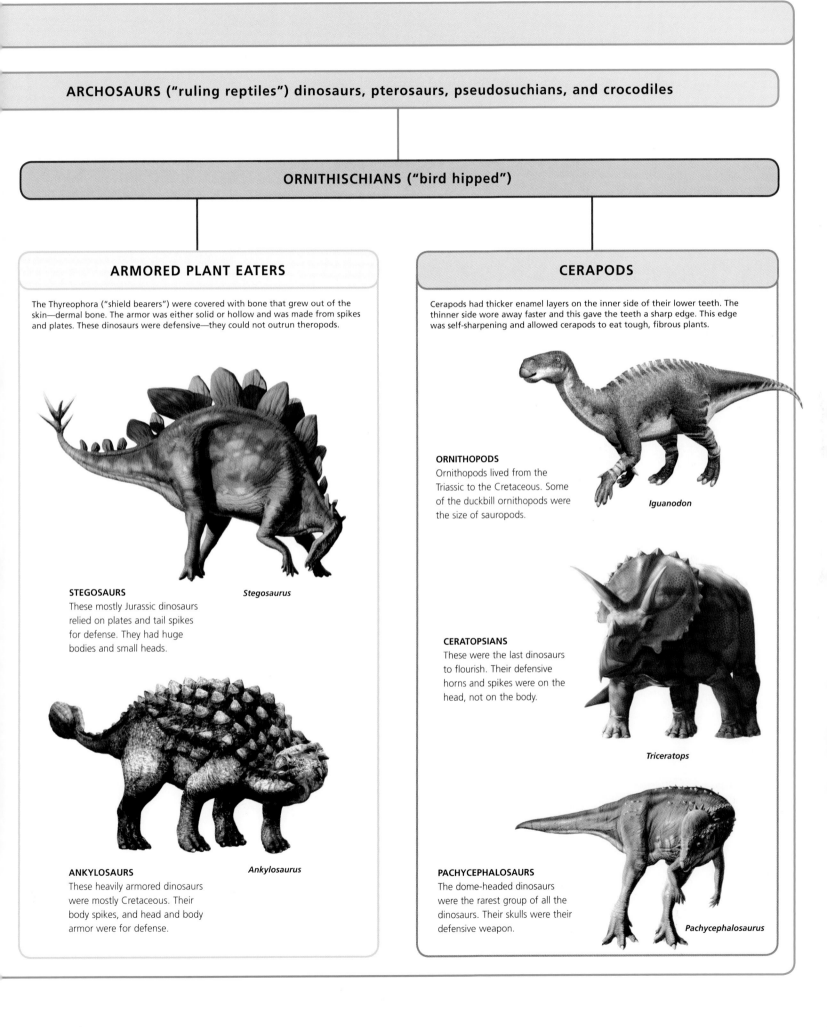

ARMORED PLANT EATERS

The Thyreophora ("shield bearers") were covered with bone that grew out of the skin—dermal bone. The armor was either solid or hollow and was made from spikes and plates. These dinosaurs were defensive—they could not outrun theropods.

Stegosaurus

STEGOSAURS
These mostly Jurassic dinosaurs relied on plates and tail spikes for defense. They had huge bodies and small heads.

Ankylosaurus

ANKYLOSAURS
These heavily armored dinosaurs were mostly Cretaceous. Their body spikes, and head and body armor were for defense.

CERAPODS

Cerapods had thicker enamel layers on the inner side of their lower teeth. The thinner side wore away faster and this gave the teeth a sharp edge. This edge was self-sharpening and allowed cerapods to eat tough, fibrous plants.

ORNITHOPODS
Ornithopods lived from the Triassic to the Cretaceous. Some of the duckbill ornithopods were the size of sauropods.

Iguanodon

CERATOPSIANS
These were the last dinosaurs to flourish. Their defensive horns and spikes were on the head, not on the body.

Triceratops

PACHYCEPHALOSAURS
The dome-headed dinosaurs were the rarest group of all the dinosaurs. Their skulls were their defensive weapon.

Pachycephalosaurus

Plant eaters

Eating plants in the Mesozoic era was not as easy as eating plants today. Most plant-eating dinosaurs ate non-flowering plants, such as cycads and conifers. These plants are much less nutritious than today's flowering plants. This is why plant-eating dinosaurs had to eat all the time and why they had such big guts—they needed to keep the plants in the gut longer to squeeze every bit of nutrition out of them. To help digest plant matter, plant eaters had a gizzard next to their stomach. So that they would not compete with each other, some ate plants only at ground level, others ate just from bushes, while the tallest dinosaurs ate from the treetops.

GINGKO
Ginkgos were common in the Jurassic. Their leaves were almost identical to the leaves of today's ginkgos.

GASTROLITHS
Some dinosaurs swallowed smooth stones (gastroliths). Their muscular gizzard crashed them together to grind the fiber-rich plant material.

Bumps

Root

OTHNIELIA
This Jurassic dinosaur ate small leaves at ground level. Some of its teeth were only ¹/₁₀ inch (3 mm) above the gum line so they ate the softest leaves they could find.

PLANT-EATER TEETH
The tooth on the left has little bumps on the edge to help cut up plants. The tooth on the right has a thick root, up to 1 inch (2.5 cm). This stopped it from being ripped out of the mouth when the dinosaur stripped leaves from branches.

TEETH AND JAWS

The earliest plant-eating dinosaurs had thick teeth covered with enamel. More advanced dinosaurs had enamel only on one side. As the teeth from the upper and lower jaws ground up the plant matter, the softer side wore away faster than the enamel. This made the teeth self-sharpening. They were also ever-growing and ever-replacing. We only get two sets of teeth in our entire lifetime, but dinosaurs got hundreds!

Horsetail

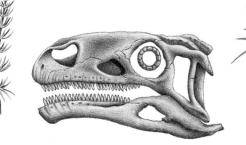

Pine cone

PLATEOSAURUS
Plateosaurus had thick teeth that could strip the hard horsetail plants.

BRACHIOSAURUS
Brachiosaurus had thin teeth with thick enamel to strip tree branches.

STEGOSAURUS FEEDING

Stegosaurus ate non-flowering plants such as cycads, conifers, and ferns. Because these plants do not regrow quickly, *Stegosaurus* was always on the move to find new plants to eat.

Magnolia

Tree fern

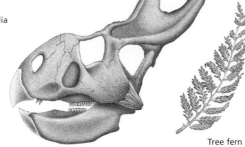

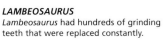

LAMBEOSAURUS
Lambeosaurus had hundreds of grinding teeth that were replaced constantly.

PROTOCERATOPS
Protoceratops had a beak like a parrot and strong jaws with chopping teeth.

HETERODONTOSAURUS
Heterodontosaurus had teeth at the front to cut plants and chopping teeth in the cheek.

Meat eaters

Meat-eating dinosaurs were designed with inbuilt weapons, including foot claws, hand claws, and teeth. There were many different kinds of teeth and claws and each had a specific job to do. The teeth had two functions—to kill and to dismember. They were constantly replaced during the life of a dinosaur as they wore out, or got pulled out. Claws also came in many shapes. Some grabbed, others tore, and the bigger ones acted like deep cutting sabers. Defenses against these weapons were based on armor, spikes, herding behavior, and simple escape.

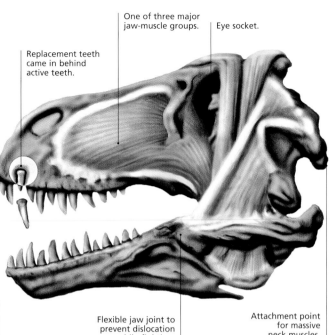

One of three major jaw-muscle groups.

Eye socket.

Replacement teeth came in behind active teeth.

Flexible jaw joint to prevent dislocation while fighting.

Attachment point for massive neck muscles.

BONE-CRUSHING JAWS
Tyrannosaurus had massively powerful jaw muscles that helped it crunch up the bones of its prey.

These teeth are curved on the front and serrated, or sawlike, on the back. Replacement teeth are waiting at the base of each tooth.

QUICK ESCAPE
Triassic meat eaters are chasing a lizard about to escape up a tree. Triassic theropods had not yet achieved their giant sizes, so any prey that could get 10 feet (3 m) off the ground was safe—unless flying pterosaurs were nearby.

TOOLS AND DIET

Teeth and claws are designed specially for particular food sources. As a general rule, the smaller the teeth, the smaller the prey—no teeth meant the dinosaur ate food that could be swallowed in one gulp. One special feature of dinosaur meat eaters was the "shock-absorber lower jaw." The lower jaw had an open joint at the back that allowed dinosaurs to pick up struggling prey without dislocating their jaws in the process.

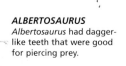

ALBERTOSAURUS
Albertosaurus had dagger-like teeth that were good for piercing prey.

OVIRAPTOR
Oviraptor had a strong beak that could break tough foods.

COMPSOGNATHUS
Compsognathus had long arms to grab small prey. It used its jaws to kill prey.

KILLING MACHINE

When it comes to two-legged mega-predators, *Tyrannosaurus* was the best-designed killing machine the world has ever seen. Its step was 13 feet (4 m) long and its huge mouth crunched down with more than 50 sharp, stabbing teeth.

DID YOU KNOW?

Tyrant is the name given to a harsh ruler, which is why *Tyrannosaurus* got its name meaning "tyrant lizard." Sometimes it is called *Tyrannosaurus rex* because *rex* is Latin for "king," so this name means "king of the tyrant lizards."

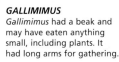

GALLIMIMUS
Gallimimus had a beak and may have eaten anything small, including plants. It had long arms for gathering.

BARYONYX
Baryonyx had a long snout and hooklike claws. It may have fished in lakes and rivers.

TYRANNOSAURUS
Tyrannosaurus was designed to rip animals apart. Each gulp sent 44 pounds (20 kg) of meat down its throat.

A Dinosaur's Anatomy

A dinosaur's anatomy was similar to many of today's land animals, but it was closest in structure to crocodiles and birds. Dinosaurs had two legs or four legs. Two-legged dinosaurs sometimes had arms for grabbing and sometimes their arms were for flying. All dinosaurs' necks had to be flexible enough to reach food and their heads had to be big enough to eat the food. Their bodies had to be big enough to process the food and breathe. Dinosaurs' legs had to be strong enough to hold their bodies off the ground and to walk fast, or to run. Their tails had to be long enough to hold the main leg muscles and possibly act as a weapon.

The organs
The organs hung from inside the rib cage and pelvis. Plant eaters needed a much larger digestive system than meat eaters. That is why most plant eaters were four-legged—to allow enough room for their large digestive system.

The skin
The skin's prime function was to protect a dinosaur against insects, predators, and the burning Mesozoic sun. Some skin had armor. Color patterns in the skin conveyed information to friends and enemies.

ANATOMY OF *GIGANOTOSAURUS*

This giant Cretaceous feeding machine was perfectly engineered to chase and attack. Its long legs gave it a stride that could outpace any plant eater. The foot claws were backed by tons of weight for maximum power. The short, powerful neck muscles allowed it to tear off chunks of meat larger than a human.

The muscles
The muscles were designed for movement and support. Dinosaurs with a lot of muscle or with thick muscle could not move as fast as leaner dinosaurs. Two-legged dinosaurs had to balance everything without falling over.

DID YOU KNOW?

Paleontologists learn a lot about extinct animals by studying living ones. For example, the legs of an ostrich are not different from a meat-eating dinosaur's. By watching ostriches walk, paleontologists can get a good idea of how meat eaters walked.

ORGANS AND MUSCLES

Every once in a great while paleontologists get lucky—dinosaur fossils sometimes preserve internal organs, muscles, and skin. Today these can be scanned with the latest technology. By looking inside with technology paleontologists do not have to spend years carefully taking away the rock that surrounds the fossils. This is important when the organs are surrounded by rock and by 13 feet (4 m) long ribs. The scan of one small meat-eater fossil, *Scipionyx,* shows the outline of a liver!

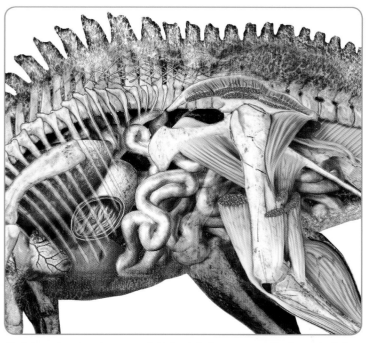

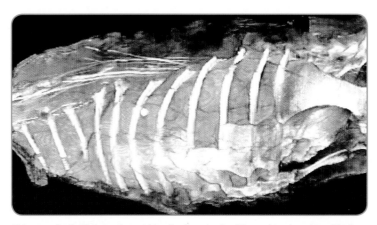

This scan of a fossil shows the outside of a rib cage, shoulder, and tendons. It could take more than five years for a paleontologist to prepare this fossil with standard techniques.

The information about the organs of this *Brachylophosaurus* was taken from a fossil that had fossilized soft tissue around its skeleton—this gave many clues to its anatomy.

The bones
Bones have roles other than weight bearing. Bones of the neck and legs are hollow in many two-legged meat eaters. This allows them to move faster. Some bones are unique and paleontologists can identify a species from just one.

"Heart"

AN UNUSUAL SPECIMEN

This fossil of *Thescelosaurus* has two surprises. The ribs have thick extensions that overlap each other, as in some birds. A large unidentified mass just below the shoulder blade was initially thought to be a "heart" but this specimen is still being studied.

Skeletons and skulls

Dinosaurs were the first land animals to walk on two legs. Two-legged dinosaurs could use their arms for food gathering or defense. Two-legged dinosaurs, such as *Hypsiliophodon*, had long legs and could run on their toes. This made them fast and they were able to turn quickly. The four-legged *Camarasaurus* is a good example of the "suspension bridge" design of a dinosaur's skeleton. The four legs bore the weight of the body and the bones in the spine were connected with fiber-like tissue and acted like bridge cables that distributed the load evenly. The backbone was not solid but had many holes to lighten the skeleton. The neck had twice as many bones as a human's, which made it more flexible than ours.

DINOSAUR SKULLS

In the skulls of plant eaters the joint between the upper and lower jaw lies below the level of the teeth. This makes the jaws come together like nut-crackers. The skulls of meat eaters have the jaw joint in line with the teeth. This makes the jaws come together like scissors, which makes for a better cut!

Ouranosaurus This plant eater had many teeth back toward its jaw joint. This gave the jaws a more powerful grinding action.

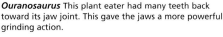

Ceratosaurus This meat eater had its teeth at the front of its mouth. The jaw muscles were designed to slam the jaws shut, putting the main force of the bite at the front.

DID YOU KNOW?

Many dinosaur skeletons mounted for display in museums are made of replica bones so that the original fossils can be studied and preserved. Dinosaur bones are replicated by making a cast that is then filled with resin or fiberglass. Replica bones are lighter and easier to move around—they are simpler to drill and mount for exhibitions.

HUGE SAUROPOD BONES
This huge sauropod thighbone from Argentina is larger than the scientists who discovered it.

Hip
The hips were fused to five bones in the spine for added strength.

Backbone
Each bone had extra tissue connections—one in the front and one behind.

Tail
Tails could have more than 50 bones. They were carried off the ground.

Hind feet
Thick pads were under the feet to absorb the weight.

Chest
The chests were barrel shaped to "hang" the guts off the ribs.

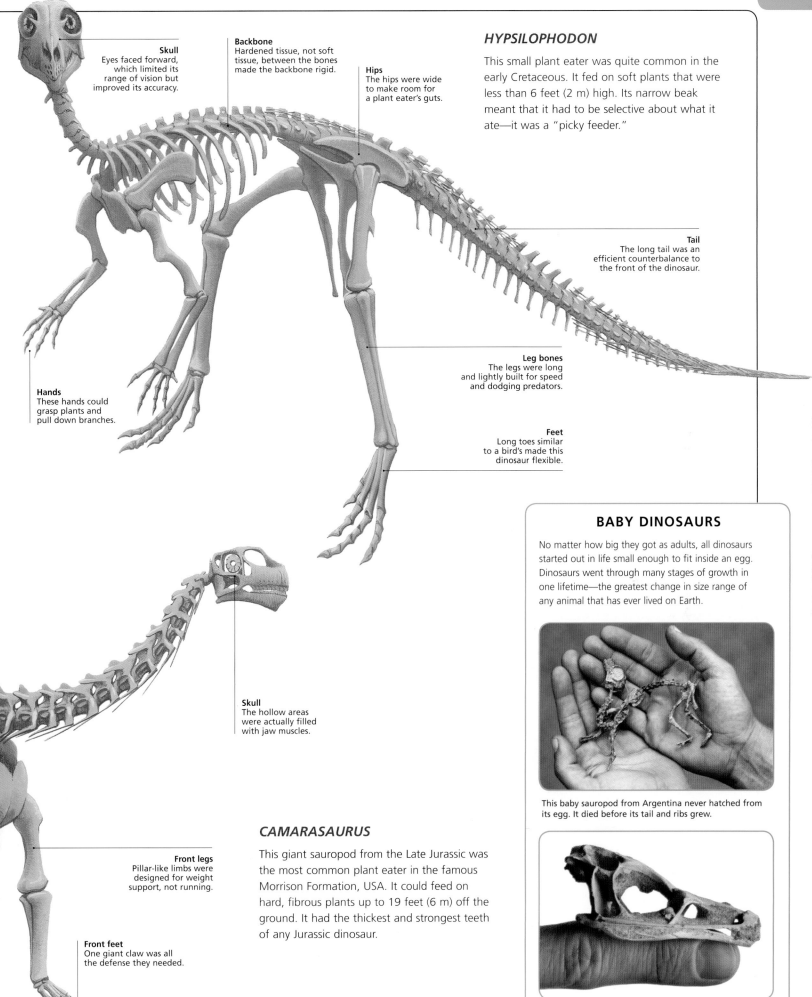

Skull
Eyes faced forward, which limited its range of vision but improved its accuracy.

Backbone
Hardened tissue, not soft tissue, between the bones made the backbone rigid.

Hips
The hips were wide to make room for a plant eater's guts.

Hands
These hands could grasp plants and pull down branches.

Leg bones
The legs were long and lightly built for speed and dodging predators.

Feet
Long toes similar to a bird's made this dinosaur flexible.

Tail
The long tail was an efficient counterbalance to the front of the dinosaur.

Skull
The hollow areas were actually filled with jaw muscles.

Front legs
Pillar-like limbs were designed for weight support, not running.

Front feet
One giant claw was all the defense they needed.

HYPSILOPHODON

This small plant eater was quite common in the early Cretaceous. It fed on soft plants that were less than 6 feet (2 m) high. Its narrow beak meant that it had to be selective about what it ate—it was a "picky feeder."

CAMARASAURUS

This giant sauropod from the Late Jurassic was the most common plant eater in the famous Morrison Formation, USA. It could feed on hard, fibrous plants up to 19 feet (6 m) off the ground. It had the thickest and strongest teeth of any Jurassic dinosaur.

BABY DINOSAURS

No matter how big they got as adults, all dinosaurs started out in life small enough to fit inside an egg. Dinosaurs went through many stages of growth in one lifetime—the greatest change in size range of any animal that has ever lived on Earth.

This baby sauropod from Argentina never hatched from its egg. It died before its tail and ribs grew.

This skull of a baby theropod has big eye sockets. Eyes grew large so the babies could see food and predators.

Brain and senses

All animals with backbones have brains that are similar in structure—they all have parts for "thinking," "feeling," moving, and sensing. Scientists get clues about the size and shape of different dinosaur brains from the size and shape of fossil skulls. The larger an animal's brain is in relation to the size of its body, the smarter it is. All dinosaurs had tiny brains compared to humans. The brain of a small meat eater was larger than the brain of a huge plant eater because a meat eater not only had to move fast to survive, it also had to hunt—it had to be smart. If a behavior or movement of a dinosaur was important, then the part of its brain that was used for that behavior or movement developed and became bigger.

Iguanodon had a good sense of smell and taste. It may have been able to smell hidden predators or distant food.

SMELL AND TASTE

Dinosaurs could probably taste the air with specialized cells in the mouth. This helped them find food and avoid predators.

BRAIN

If you compare a mammal and a dinosaur of the same size, the brain of a mammal is relatively larger. Mammals are much smarter than dinosaurs. Some dinosaurs had brains that were almost as big as the brains of some birds.

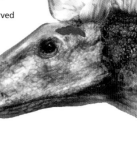

Stegosaurus had a famously small brain—the smallest of any ornithischian—but it served it well for millions of years.

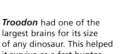

Troodon had one of the largest brains for its size of any dinosaur. This helped it survive as a fast hunter.

SIGHT

Most plant eaters had eyes that faced different directions, which gave them a wide field of vision. Many meat eaters had eyes that faced forward, which gave them a limited field of vision but increased accuracy and depth-perception.

Fossils of *Troodon* show that it had large eyes, which led scientists to believe that it had good eyesight.

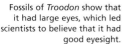

Saurolophus made honking sounds, so its hearing was probably good enough to hear the replies.

HEARING

Dinosaurs have one large ear bone and can hear low-frequency sounds. Mammals have three small ear bones and can hear high-frequency sounds. It is possible that dinosaurs could hear frequencies too low for humans, as crocodiles can.

Humans have the largest brain of all terrestrial animals. A human head is mostly brain.

Iguanodon **brain**
This cast of an *Iguanodon* brain shows the size of each specialized part.

TOUCH

Touch was the least important sense for dinosaurs. Most of their skin was too thick and lacked the ability to touch and feel that humans have.

Fossilized dinosaur skin is a rare find. It shows us that dinosaurs had thick scaly skin that would have had little sense of touch.

HOW DID DINOSAURS COMMUNICATE?

COMMUNICATION

Communication is important for all animals. Messages can range from "I have found food" to "There is a *Tyrannosaurus rex* behind those trees!" Long-distance communication was probably conveyed with sound. Closer communication was probably conveyed more with sight. Color patterns were also important. Color can convey messages such as "I will defend this territory" or "It is mating season."

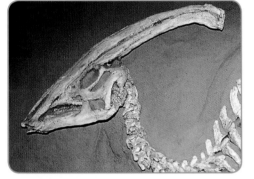

This skull of *Parasaurolophus* has a crest made from the "upper lip bone" and the nasal bone.

Call This two-legged ornithopod, a pachycephalosaur, used its mouth to create a specific call.

Notes Hadrosaurs, or duckbilled dinosaurs, used their crests to mimic specific sounds and series of notes.

Honk Some dinosaurs without hollow crests had an inflatable sac that they used for honking.

Air chamber

SENDING SIGNALS

This non-crested hadrosaur is using an inflatable nasal sac like a musical reed instrument. It could make different sounds by tightening the muscles around its nostrils. The shape and color of the nasal sac also conveyed information.

Deflated nasal sac

Inflated nasal sac

PARASAUROLOPHUS'S HOLLOW CREST

Inside the crest of this hadrosaur is a long air chamber lined with nasal tissue. The greatly expanded nasal chamber could humidify air, increase the sense of smell, and produce sounds like a one-note Mesozoic trombone.

Digestion

Dinosaurs evolved specialized teeth, jaws, and guts to get the most nutrition from their food. *Tyrannosaurus* took huge bites of meat and did not chew, so it needed a large stomach to hold the chunks of meat while they were being digested. *Apatosaurus* was a plant eater, it stripped cycads, conifers, and gingkos and the unchewed food was ground up in the gizzard by stones that it swallowed. The stomach and intestines finished off the digestion of the plants—meat eaters did not need intestines as large as those of plant eaters. Undigested food came out as dung—a fossilized pellet of dung is called a coprolite.

DID YOU KNOW?

Some of the most interesting dinosaur fossils are dung fossils, or coprolites. Coprolites give scientists clues to what dinosaurs ate, and how their digestion worked. Coprolites come in all shapes and sizes and can contain bits and pieces of seeds, pinecones, plant stems, and even crushed bones.

INSIDE *APATOSAURUS*

It took a long time to digest conifers and cycads, so the guts had to be big, and long. The longer the plants spent inside the guts, the more nutrients could be extracted. A 108-foot (33-m) sauropod may have had more than 328 feet (100 m) of guts.

Grinding stones

Saltasaurus is stripping branches from a tree. These dinosaurs did not chew plants. Their teeth acted only as prongs on a rake that gathered plants.

GRINDING STONES
Both modern birds and dinosaurs are known to have swallowed stones to help the digestion of tough plants. The constant churning of the stomach made the stones smash together and grind up the plants. During this process the stones became smooth and polished—they looked like pebbles.

Many polished pebbles look like stomach stones, but only the ones found inside the rib cage of a dinosaur can truly be called gastroliths.

DIGESTING MEAT

Plant eaters' digestion is not as efficient as meat eaters'. This is why plant-eating dinosaurs had to eat so much. Meat eaters also digest their food more quickly than plant eaters, which is why meat eaters had to eat more often. In some modern birds meat can pass entirely through their digestive systems in just hours.

In the stomach of this *Coelophysis* fossil are the remains of its last meal—a small reptile fossil.

Small lizards and mammals made a tasty snack for meat-eating dinosaurs during the Cretaceous period.

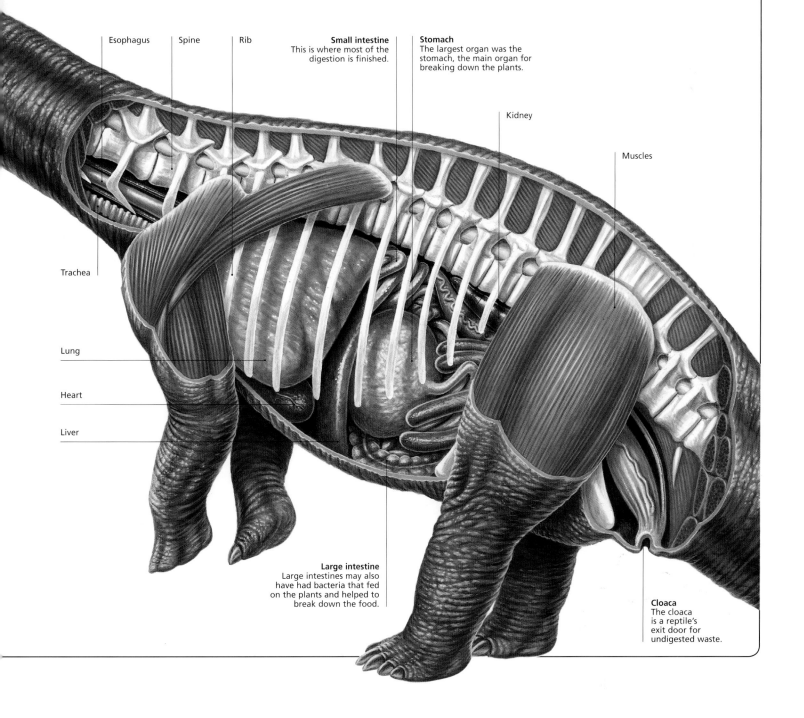

Esophagus

Spine

Rib

Small intestine
This is where most of the digestion is finished.

Stomach
The largest organ was the stomach, the main organ for breaking down the plants.

Kidney

Muscles

Trachea

Lung

Heart

Liver

Large intestine
Large intestines may also have had bacteria that fed on the plants and helped to break down the food.

Cloaca
The cloaca is a reptile's exit door for undigested waste.

Regulating temperature

We do not know whether dinosaurs were "warm-blooded" or "cold-blooded"—or somewhere in between. A "warm-blooded" animal controls its body temperature and keeps it constant in the same way that birds and mammals do. A "cold-blooded" animal has a varying body temperature and controls it with external means—such as the sun— in the same way that lizards, snakes, and crocodiles do. In today's world, temperature regulating usually means keeping heat inside the body. In the world of the dinosaurs, it often meant getting rid of heat. The Mesozoic was hot and a giant dinosaur could cook in the sun if it did not shed excess heat.

OURANOSAURUS SAIL

The sail on *Ouranosaurus* was 3 feet (1 m) tall. It was used to regulate temperature, to display threat, and for recognition. It also made *Ouranosaurus* look much bigger than it actually was, which was important when hungry theropods were around.

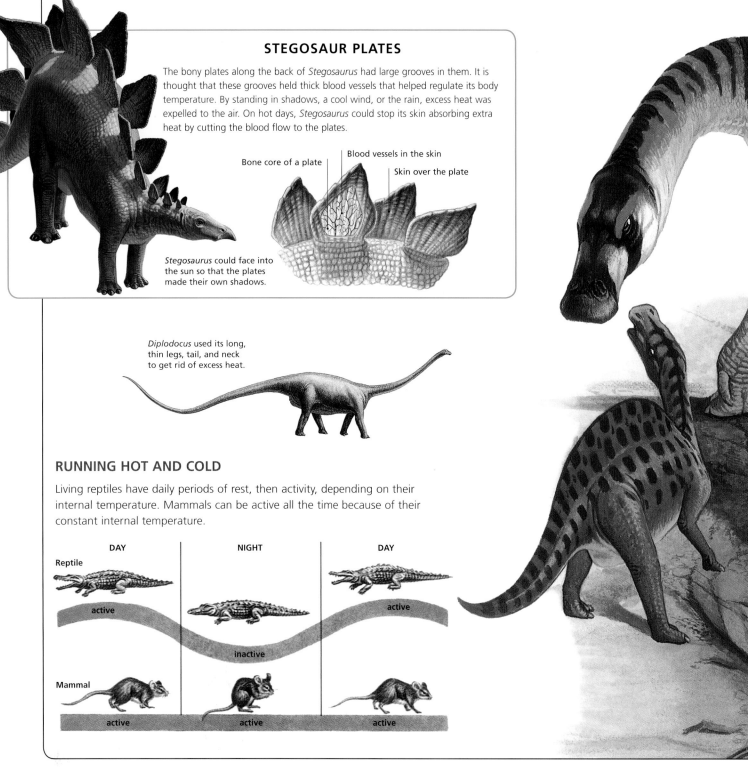

STEGOSAUR PLATES

The bony plates along the back of *Stegosaurus* had large grooves in them. It is thought that these grooves held thick blood vessels that helped regulate its body temperature. By standing in shadows, a cool wind, or the rain, excess heat was expelled to the air. On hot days, *Stegosaurus* could stop its skin absorbing extra heat by cutting the blood flow to the plates.

Bone core of a plate

Blood vessels in the skin

Skin over the plate

Stegosaurus could face into the sun so that the plates made their own shadows.

Diplodocus used its long, thin legs, tail, and neck to get rid of excess heat.

RUNNING HOT AND COLD

Living reptiles have daily periods of rest, then activity, depending on their internal temperature. Mammals can be active all the time because of their constant internal temperature.

DAY

NIGHT

DAY

Reptile

active

active

inactive

Mammal

active

active

active

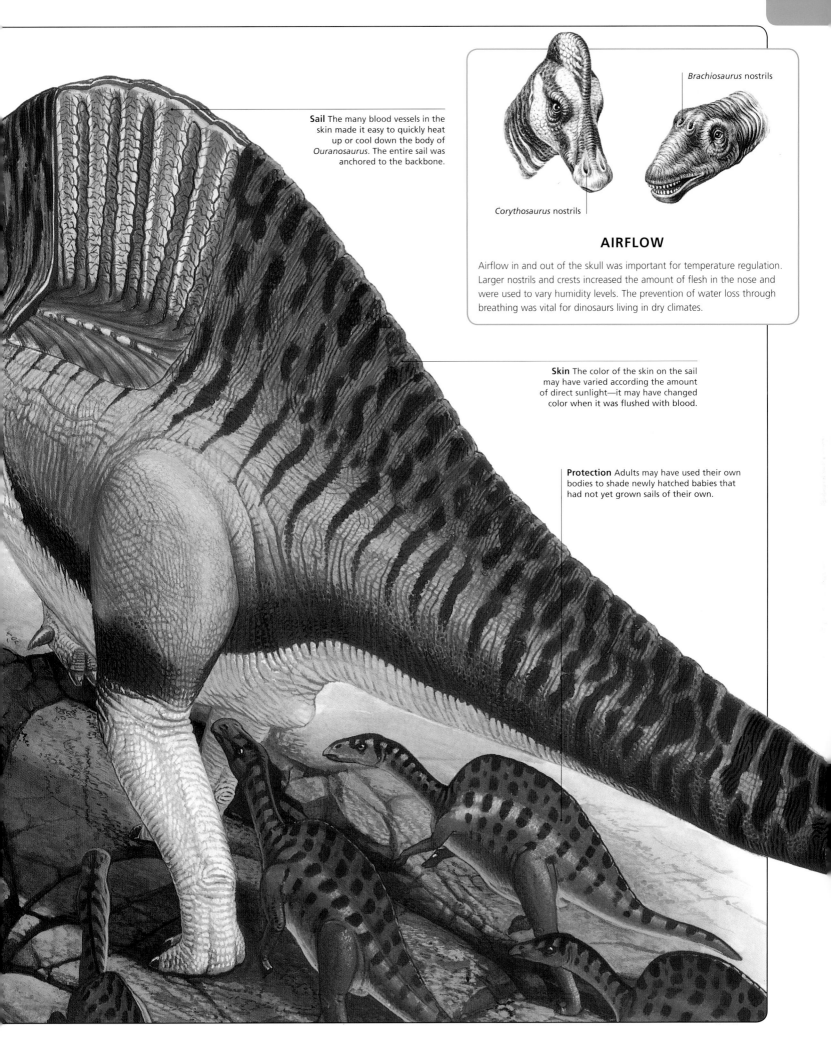

Sail The many blood vessels in the skin made it easy to quickly heat up or cool down the body of *Ouranosaurus*. The entire sail was anchored to the backbone.

Brachiosaurus nostrils

Corythosaurus nostrils

AIRFLOW

Airflow in and out of the skull was important for temperature regulation. Larger nostrils and crests increased the amount of flesh in the nose and were used to vary humidity levels. The prevention of water loss through breathing was vital for dinosaurs living in dry climates.

Skin The color of the skin on the sail may have varied according the amount of direct sunlight—it may have changed color when it was flushed with blood.

Protection Adults may have used their own bodies to shade newly hatched babies that had not yet grown sails of their own.

The Next Generation

Dinosaurs had a variety of nesting behaviors. Some nests were isolated and others were laid in groups close to each other. Some nests were filled with eggs that were arranged into patterns and some were not in nests at all but were scattered around on the ground. Some adult dinosaurs cared for their young more than any living reptiles do—more like birds do. Some may have abandoned their eggs in the way that some lizards and turtles do today. The surprising thing is that dinosaur eggs were not big when compared to a dinosaur's body size. Scientists have found hundreds of sites that contain nests, eggs, babies, and adults.

DEPENDENT PLANT EATER
Born with weak bones, plant eaters were looked after until they were strong enough to leave.

INDEPENDENT MEAT EATER
When a hungry meat-eating theropod hatched from its egg it was probably ready to walk straightaway.

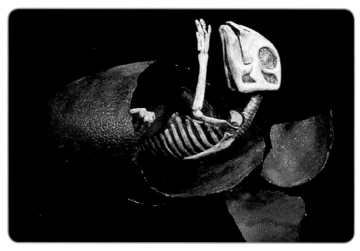

BABY BONES This duckbill baby fossil was found in Montana, USA. There was no space inside the egg for a dinosaur with the same proportions as an adult. Its skull, neck, and tail grew out after it hatched. The young were protected until they were able to feed and defend themselves—or until they were fast enough to escape danger.

DIFFERENT EGGS

Chicken Compare the size of this chicken egg with the size of dinosaur eggs.

Velociraptor *Velociraptor* and most theropods had elongated eggs.

Oviraptor *Oviraptor* eggs were long and thin with bumps on the shell.

Hypselosaurus
Hypselosaurus eggs as big as footballs have been found in France.

Sauropod
Spherical sauropod eggs are the largest eggs found.

EGG-LAYING PATTERNS

Dinosaurs laid their eggs in many different ways. Some made nests, lined them to keep the eggs warm, and laid their eggs in a particular pattern. Some seemed to have laid them on the ground in no pattern. Only a few examples of the many patterns of egg laying are shown here.

Plant-eating sauropods laid their eggs in an arc shape across the ground.

Hadrosaurs laid their eggs in a spiral pattern in a shallow, lined nest.

Some small meat eaters laid their eggs side by side to form two rows in the nest.

No one knows which dinosaur made this nest. The eggs were scattered.

A MOTHER'S CARE

RAISING A FAMILY

Some plant eaters cared for their newly hatched young for weeks until they could walk. During that time the hatchlings depended entirely on their parents for food and for protection from predators. Parents probably foraged and partly digested the food before they fed it to their young. Large herds of *Maiasaura* built their nests close together. They tended to their young in the nest for six to eight weeks until the hatchlings' bones slowly hardened and grew strong enough for them to walk. Small meat-eating dinosaurs grew more quickly and could probably run soon after hatching.

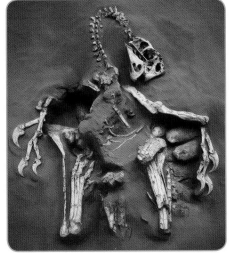

This nest was found in the Gobi Desert, Mongolia. It shows an *Oviraptor* lying on top of the nest with two eggs underneath its elbow.

Maiasaura nests contained up to 25 eggs. The nest was scooped out of mud in the shape of a bowl. The name *Maiasaura* means "good mother lizard."

FEEDING TIME

An adult *Oviraptor* brings food to its hatchlings. This meal could have been a lizard or a young plant-eating dinosaur. A young *Oviraptor* was too small to hunt anything except insects.

Living in a Herd

Some plant-eating dinosaurs, such as sauropods, hadrosaurs, and ceratopsians, or horned dinosaurs, lived in herds that protected their young from preying meat eaters. It was safer to move around in large groups than to travel in small groups or alone. Scientists have found fossilized footprints, called trackways, that show meat-eating dinosaurs following herds of plant eaters. If young, sick, or weak animals became isolated from the group, they were vulnerable to attack. Plant eaters were a good source of food—one sauropod could feed a meat eater for a week.

MOVING ON

A pack of theropods from the late Jurassic stalk a herd of long-necked sauropods. The young dinosaurs have moved inside the group for protection. Large plant eaters such as *Diplodocus* ate so much that they had to continually move to find new sources of food.

Sauropod

PROTECTING THE YOUNG

Triceratops was probably the most common dinosaur in North America during the late Cretaceous. It lived in large herds and adults formed a protective ring around their young when they were threatened. *Triceratops* was not a fast mover. It had solidly built front limbs, which were shorter than its hind limbs. The skull bone was extra thick at the base of its horns and was strong enough to ram the legs of a tyrannosaur.

This scene shows a family group of *Triceratops*, perhaps part of a large herd, being threatened by a predator. The adult *Triceratops* are threatening the attacker.

Theropod

EVIDENCE OF HERDS

This photograph (below) shows fossil footprints from a herd of late Jurassic sauropods. The illustration on the left is based on the information paleontologists got from studying these fossils. Scientists use footprints to estimate the speed and direction animals were traveling.

Predators and Scavengers

There were three ways meat-eating dinosaurs could get a meal. They could find it, steal it, or kill it. Most meat eaters were predators and scavengers—it depended on the opportunities that arose. It was much easier and safer for a dinosaur to eat a carcass, or dead body, than to hunt and kill its food. The larger and slower a meat eater was, the more time it spent scavenging. A large carcass could feed many animals. When the biggest and strongest predators finished eating, the smaller scavengers fought over the leftovers. Even small animals, such as birds, pterosaurs, and young dinosaurs, could eat a whole carcass. If the body was not buried quickly it rotted and wore away. Only animals that were buried quickly were likely to become fossilized.

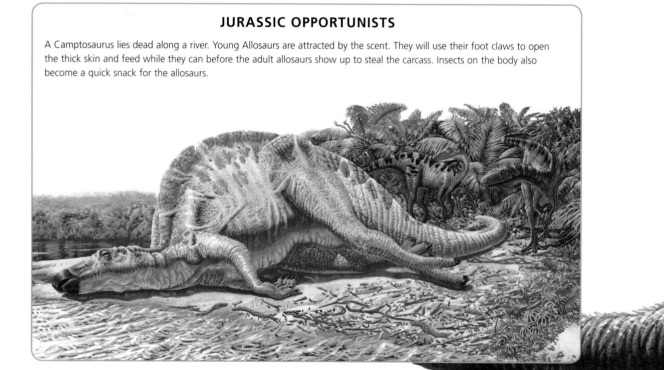

JURASSIC OPPORTUNISTS

A Camptosaurus lies dead along a river. Young Allosaurs are attracted by the scent. They will use their foot claws to open the thick skin and feed while they can before the adult allosaurs show up to steal the carcass. Insects on the body also become a quick snack for the allosaurs.

A CRETACEOUS BATTLE

A pack of *Deinonychus,* meat-eating theropods, attack a *Tenontosaurus,* an ornithopod. One theropod has been trampled and will soon die from its injuries. The rest go for *Tenontosaurus*'s neck and body, its least defended parts. This scene is based on a fossil find in the USA.

Tenontosaurus

Deinonychus

Methods of Survival

Dinosaurs had to survive a world full of dangers. They had to find enough food to eat and, at the same time, protect themselves from being eaten. Plant eaters were better defenders than meat eaters. They protected themselves with horns, armor, and spikes—and by living in herds. Meat eaters were usually the attackers and they needed to capture and kill their food. They used claws and teeth to kill their prey. When meat eaters were attacked they used their speed, claws, and teeth for defense.

Diplodocus

CERATOSAURUS MEETS *DIPLODOCUS*

Diplodocus uses its long, thick tail like a whip. The weight and power of its tail is enough to completely knock over a 20-foot (6-m) long *Ceratosaurus*—and break its ribs in the process.

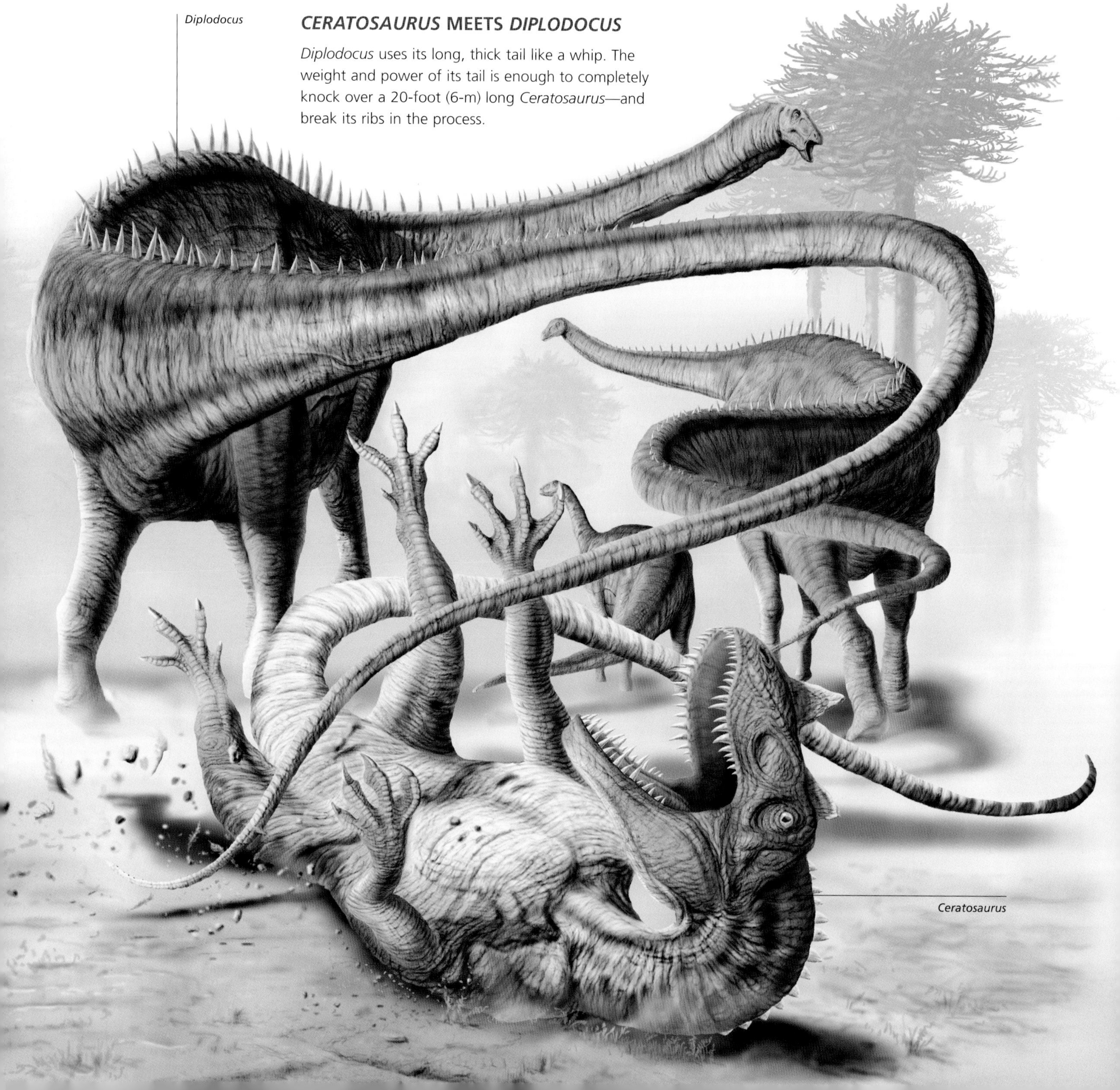

Ceratosaurus

ATTACK

The best weapons are well designed and powerful. Teeth, clawed hands, and clawed feet were a dinosaur's inbuilt weapons. Their power depended on the size of the dinosaur behind them. For example, an adult *Deinonychus* was more dangerous than a young tyrannosaur of the same size. This is because *Deinonychus* had clawed hands and tyrannosaurs did not. Some dinosaurs had thin jaws to deliver precise cuts; others were massive body rippers like *Giganotosaurus*.

Velociraptor This was a small dinosaur—smaller than a human—but it was quick and it had deadly sickle-shaped claws.

Baryonyx This giant predator had massive crocodile-like jaws that could slam shut at great speed.

Giganotosaurus This huge dinosaur had 8-inch (20-cm) long serrated, or sawlike, teeth that sliced through its victims' hides.

Deinonychus This dinosaur had a claw that acted as a powerful weapon. It used its razor-sharp teeth to dismember prey.

DEFENSE

Herding behavior was the best defense for many dinosaurs but, when it came to one-on-one battle, they used their armor and spikes effectively. Plant eaters did not have to kill their attackers, they just had to make it too painful for them to continue fighting.

Ankylosaurus The entire top of this dinosaur was covered with thick armor. There was nothing an attacker could bite into without breaking its teeth.

Pachycephalosaurus This dinosaur had a dome of solid bone on its head that it used as a battering ram. It could break a tyrannosaur's ribs.

Triceratops With horns more than 3 feet (1 m) long, this dinosaur could pierce a tyrannosaur's legs.

Iguanodon *Iguanodon*'s spiked thumb was not large but it was backed up by the weight of a dinosaur almost the same size as an elephant. This gave it enough power to poke the eye out of a theropod.

Size and strength

There are certain things that happen to all animals as they get bigger. The heavier they get, the more energy they need to move. The larger the animal, the more they can hurt themselves if they fall down. It also gets harder for them to cool down when they move fast. Two-legged animals are always smaller than four-legged animals because two legs cannot bear as much weight as four legs can. There is a stage an animal reaches when it can walk fast, with one leg on the ground at all times, but it cannot run with all legs off the ground. An example of this in today's world is the difference between rhinos and elephants—rhinos can run but elephants cannot.

SPEED

There is a simple way to tell how fast a dinosaur could have run. If its thighbone was as long as its shinbone, then it could move fast. If the thighbone had bumps and knobs, for the insertion of muscles, then it had a powerful leg and could run fast. No dinosaur was as fast as the fastest living mammal but, in the Mesozoic world, dinosaurs were the fastest animals on Earth.

The legs of an ostrich are better designed for speed than *Struthiomimus* legs.

The legs of *Struthiomimus* were not up to modern standards but they could outpace a tyrannosaur.

BIGGEST PREDATOR

If "big" means massive, then *Tyrannosaurus rex* wins. If "big" means longest, then *Giganotosaurus* or *Spinosaurus* wins. They are the "biggest of the big," so far.

LONGEST

Amphicoelias could have been the longest dinosaur at 196 feet (50 m) long, but the bone that was found in the late 1800s is now missing. The next longest, but with a more complete skeleton, is *Argentinosaurus*.

HEAVIEST

Argentinosaurus and *Sauroposeidon* are both estimated to have weighed more than 50 metric tons.

Argentinosaurus weighed the same as 15 African elephants!

DID YOU KNOW?

Mammals grow to a certain size and then stop. However, dinosaurs have "indeterminate growth"—they keep growing for as long as they are healthy. We may never find the "biggest" dinosaur to have ever lived.

SMALLEST

Newly hatched two-legged plant eaters would fit in the palm of a child's hand. *Micropachycephalosaurus* (below) was one of the smallest plant eaters—it was only 1½ feet (0.5 m) long. *Compsognathus* (below right) was one of the smallest meat eaters. It was only 3 feet (1 m) long and about the same height as a chicken.

Micropachycephalosaurus

Compsognathus

Skin and color

Dinosaur skin had to be thick enough to protect against insect bites, scrapes, borings, and drillings from insects. It also had to be flexible and bend while dinosaurs moved. Dinosaur skin probably changed color, which allowed them to communicate with other dinosaurs and predators. Although color is not preserved in the fossil record, scientists can find clues by looking at large animals living today.

Bone strength Most bone plates in dinosaur skin were near the backbone. Thick nodules of bone helped to strengthen the skin.

Flexible skin As the bone plates get closer to the belly they get smaller and the skin gets more flexible. This allows the belly to bulge with food.

STRIPES

Stripes are a form of camouflage and help break up an animal's outline. Stripe patterns may have indicated a dinosaur's age.

SPOTS

Spots are another way to blend into the background. Some animals can deepen their color if they have specialized skin cells.

DULL

Dull is sometimes the best defense. Most large plant eaters blended with their environment's shades of browns and grays.

COLORS AND MARKINGS

Although we do not know what colors dinosaurs were, we can take some guesses. Maybe the frill of a horned dinosaur had circles like a bull's eye to look bigger and frighten predators. Or maybe it was colorful to attract mates. Perhaps it was drab, for good camouflage.

| A threatening display? | Attraction by color? | Dull to blend into surroundings? |

CREATIVE COLOR

Scientists do not know what color dinosaurs were. Some paleontologists believe plant-eating dinosaurs had dull colors to hide from predators. Meat-eating dinosaurs may have been dull colored as well, in order to hide and ambush plant eaters. Other scientists think plant eaters, such as the duckbilled dinosaurs pictured below, changed color to mate or to defend their territories.

Armor, plates, and horns

All ornithischian ("bird-hipped") dinosaurs were plant eaters. They all needed a defense against faster meat eaters. By the end of the Mesozoic they had evolved with the most advanced system of armor that any animal has ever had. The best examples of these defenses are spikes on stegosaurs and ceratopsians, armor on ankylosaurs, plates on stegosaurs, and small bone patches in the skin—osteoderms—which were found in all ornithischians. The armor was rigid or flexible, and solid or hollow. It grew on the dinosaur where it may have been exposed and vulnerable to attack. The main purpose was to make the plant eater look bigger and more threatening. If that failed it could protect the victim and cause a great deal of damage to the attacker.

A full-grown *Stegosaurus* had 17 plates and four tail spikes.

KEEPING COOL

Stegosaurus was equipped with plates along each side of its backbone from its neck down to the middle of its tail. They were used for defense and they were probably also used for regulating the body temperature of the dinosaur.

The skin on the outside of *Stegosaurus* plates may have been able to change color and act as a warning to potential predators.

BUILT FOR DEFENSE

Ankylosaurs had armored defense millions of years before it was "reinvented" by the army. *Euoplocephalus* had armor, shoulder spikes, and a tail club. Each armor plate was designed to be biteproof. To be able to grow so much bone ankylosaurs needed lots of calcium. They could have eaten insects to supplement the calcium in their diet.

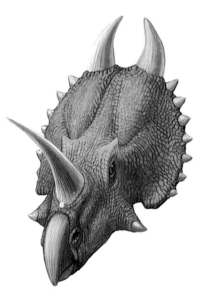

Euoplocephalus had head armor fused to its skull. To make it lighter, it had eight cavities in its head.

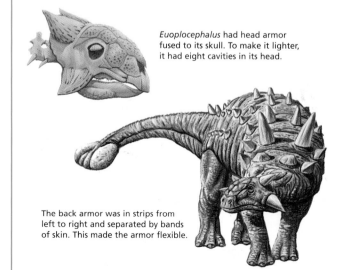

The back armor was in strips from left to right and separated by bands of skin. This made the armor flexible.

Nasal horns Centrosaurine horned dinosaurs had nasal horns and frill spikes with small frill shields.

Brow horns Chasmosaurine horned dinosaurs had brow horns, fewer and smaller frill spikes and larger frill shields.

TRICERATOPS

The last plant eater to fight a *Tyrannosaurus rex* was *Triceratops*. Its brow horns protected its jaw muscles at the base of the frill and could spear the leg of a tyrannosaur. The longest known horn is more than 3 feet (1 m).

Claws and spikes

Claws and spikes were mostly used for attack and defense. Dinosaur claws came in many shapes and sizes. They were thin, thick, short, long, straight, and curved. Foot claws were dangerous because they had a lot of muscle power behind them. Attacking hand claws would have been terrifying when a dinosaur reared up on its hind legs. The most effective spikes were ones that looked so scary they made a predator look elsewhere for a meal. Spikes that grew on the shoulder or the tail and moved like spears were used actively for defense.

Utahraptor was a birdlike theropod with a 9-inch (23-cm) sickle-shape claw on each foot. Its feet were its main weapons.

Not all claws were used for attack or defense. *Mononykus* was a small theropod with one claw on the end of each short arm. These may have been used to dig up termite mounds.

Allosaurus was a powerful predator. It had three fingers on each hand, which ended in large, hooked claws. This dinosaur hunted small plant eaters and, occasionally, a sauropod.

DEADLY WEAPON

Dacentrurus, a stegosaur, was a moving fort. The longest spikes were designed to pierce deeply into a predator. *Dacentrurus* did not have to kill, it just had to disable. Its shoulder and tail spikes were at the same level as the legs of a large predator. It only had to damage one leg of an attacker and the fight was over.

TEETH

Dinosaur teeth had two main parts—the root and the crown. The crown was made of hard enamel on the outside and a softer lining on the inside. Meat eaters' teeth had long roots and plant eaters' had short roots. Teeth were continually replaced throughout a dinosaur's life—which also meant cavities did not have time to form.

Crown

Root

These giant adult tyrannosaur teeth had roots three times longer than the crowns. This kept them anchored in the jaw and stopped them being ripped out during a fight.

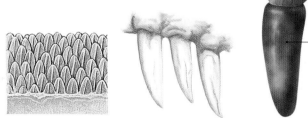

Plant-eating hadrosaurs' teeth (left) were interlocked. Theropod teeth (middle) were like daggers, spaced apart so they could cut meat. *Plateosaurus's* teeth (right) were sawlike—they had bumps along the edges to cut rough plant material.

Discovering Dinosaurs

Becoming a Fossil

Fossils are essential for studying dinosaurs but only a small percentage of animals become fossilized. Animals begin to decay quickly after death and scavengers, predators, insects, and the weather all help to increase the rate of decay. The best fossils come from animals that were buried quickly and surrounded by finely grained earth. If the rocks containing the fossil wear away or if the fossil is buried too deeply, it may never be found.

EASY MEAL

A dinosaur has just died. Two pterosaurs land on its foot and look for parasites, insects, and pieces of meat. Meat-eating theropods have not yet discovered the carcass. If they do, not much will be left. This dinosaur has died on a flood plain, so a rainstorm might cover it with sand and silt and preserve it.

FOSSIL CLUES

If the bones of a dinosaur are found in the same position they were in life, they are said to be "in articulation," and scientists can study how the animal was designed and how it moved. We can also study any injuries or diseases the animal may have had: this is called "paleopathology," the science of ancient diseases and injuries. This duckbill dinosaur skeleton is in articulation.

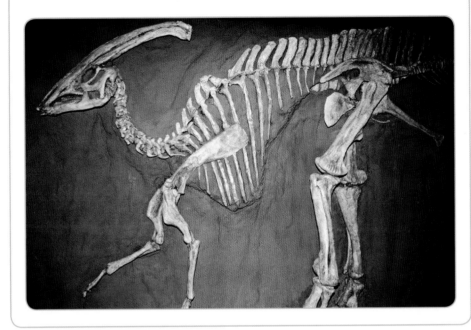

All that is left of this fish is a thin layer of carbon, which is a charcoal-like substance. All the body parts have decayed, leaving just this layer.

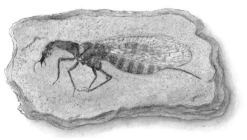

This insect fossil is an impression. The stain on the rock has the shape of the fossil but the body parts have decayed.

Precious find
Eric is a small pliosaur whose skeleton has been preserved in opal. Stones and the bones of a small fish were found inside its stomach.

DID YOU KNOW?

This famous fossil, named Eric, was found in Queensland, Australia. It is one of the most spectacular fossils in the world. As the bones decayed, they were replaced by minerals that formed a precious stone called opal.

HOW A DINOSAUR FOSSIL IS FORMED

Fossils do not form easily or quickly. Many things have to happen in a particular order for an animal to become fossilized. There are different kinds of fossils, such as bone, footprints, impressions, mineral remains, natural casts, and, rarely, "mummies," in which organs are perserved. Less than one percent of all fossils are complete animal skeletons.

DEATH
A dinosaur dies and the body is buried or washed into a river before it is completely destroyed. Usually the flesh rots away or is eaten; only the skeleton remains.

BURIAL
Layers of finely grained sand and mud cover the carcass. New layers added on top help stabilize the fossil and protect it from more decay and being washed away.

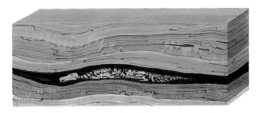

FOSSILIZATION
The sand and mud that surround the animal harden and its bones are replaced by minerals to form rock-hard fossils. This process takes thousands of years.

REDISCOVERY
Movements in Earth lift up the fossil and bring it close to the surface. The surface wears away and the fossil is exposed. If it is not found it may disappear in just one year.

Looking for Evidence

The most common dinosaur fossils are bones and teeth. Sometimes paleontologists find footprints, eggs, and dung. Complete skeletons are rare. Fossilized bones and teeth tell us much about how dinosaurs looked and how they lived. Adult bones give us clues to what they ate, what injuries they had, and how they died. Scientists use evidence to piece together information. Remains of nests, fossils of eggs, and even baby dinosaur fossils help them discover how small these babies were when they hatched and how quickly they grew.

Healed break

Bones Fossils can tell us what illnesses, accidents, and injuries a dinosaur had. This bone is from an *Iguanodon* with a fractured hip. It shows a bulge of new bone around the fracture.

Complete skeleton Complete skeletons provide more information than bones and teeth. This *Triceratops* skeleton clearly shows its solid frill and horns.

Feathers Even though fossils of feathers are rare, when they are found they often shed new light on how various dinosaurs were related to birds.

Theropod teeth

Teeth Paleontologists can tell a lot from dinosaur teeth—these sharp, sawlike teeth belonged to a powerful meat eater.

Embryos Fossilized embryos reveal clues to dinosaur life cycles, development, and behavior.

Eggs By studying nest fossils, scientists have found that dinosaur nesting behavior is similar to that of modern birds.

Bones Individual bones are the most common find and sometimes they are the missing piece of a puzzle. These dinosaur bones are still stuck in rock.

Coprolites Dinosaur dung turns into fossils as hard as rock, called coprolites. Scientists study them to learn what dinosaurs ate and how their digestive system worked.

Gastroliths Plant-eating dinosaurs swallowed stones, called gastroliths, to grind up food in their stomach. Gastroliths help scientists study dinosaur digestion.

FOOTPRINTS

MAKING TRACKS

Dinosaur footprints tell scientists a lot about how dinosaurs behaved. They give us clues as to how far and how fast they traveled, and who they traveled with. From their tracks we know that some lived in huge herds, while others traveled alone. Scientists estimate the size of a dinosaur and how fast it walked by measuring the length of the animal's stride and the size of its feet.

CARNOSAUR PRINTS
Large meat eaters walked on two legs. Each foot had three large toes and a claw.

COELUROSAUR PRINTS
Small meat eaters left footprints with slender toe marks that look like birds' footprints.

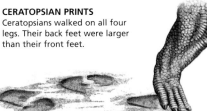

CERATOPSIAN PRINTS
Ceratopsians walked on all four legs. Their back feet were larger than their front feet.

SAUROPOD PRINTS
Sauropods walked on all four feet. Their back feet made huge footprints that were almost circular.

Theropods walked on their large back feet. This Jurassic footprint was found in in Arizona, USA.

MUD TRACKS

Small plant eaters run from a meat-eating predator and leave their footprints behind in the soft mud. The riverbank is covered in prints and this is the perfect place for them to be preserved.

Fossil Sites

There are thousands of sites around the world containing all kinds of fossils. Since the 1870s, specimens have been found in Africa, America, Australia, Canada, China, and Mongolia. Everything scientists know about dinosaurs has come from fossils and there are many dinosaur bones that are yet to be discovered. Today people collect fossils as a hobby—they collect bones, teeth, plants, and shells. However, they are not just pretty rocks, they need care and preservation and they are never collected without permission. Some sites offer classes and instructions on how to dig up and care for fossils.

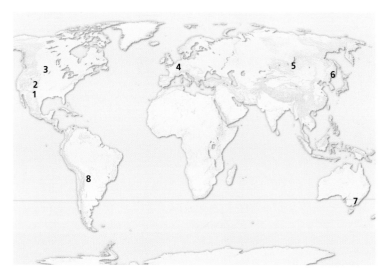

DINOSAURS AROUND THE WORLD
This map shows the eight major sites pictured but there are thousands of dinosaur sites around the world. At some places bones are not being excavated because of political unrest, lack of money, or lack of easy access—one site is only 100 miles (170 km) from the South Pole, which makes it very hard to get to.

1 DINOSAUR NATIONAL MONUMENT, UTAH, USA
This late Jurassic site was discovered in 1909 when paleontologist Earl Douglass, from the Carnegie Museum of Natural History, Pennsylvania, noticed the skeleton of a sauropod sticking out of an exposed sandstone ledge. Important fossils found here include the most complete skeleton of *Apatosaurus* ever to be discovered, as well as nearly complete skeletons of *Allosaurus*, *Dryosaurus*, and *Stegosaurus*.

2 HELL CREEK, MONTANA, USA
In 1902, paleontologist Barnum Brown, from the American Museum of Natural History, New York, began searching the Hell Creek area for dinosaur fossils. At this late Cretaceous site Brown discovered the first, incomplete, *Tyrannosaurus* skeleton. Dinosaur fossils found at Hell Creek include *Albertosaurus*, *Ankylosaurus*, *Ornithomimus*, *Pachycephalosaurus*, *Stegoceras*, *Torosaurus*, and *Troodon*.

3 DINOSAUR PROVINCIAL PARK, ALBERTA, CANADA
The history of this late Cretaceous park dates back to 1909, when a rancher, John Wagner, discovered dinosaur bones on his property. Early finds included complete skeletons of *Centrosaurus*, *Corythosaurus*, *Prosaurolophus*, and *Struthiomimus*. Scientists have found about 250 dinosaur skeletons from 36 different species, including *Edmontonia*, *Euoplocephalus*, *Lambeosaurus*, *Struthiomimus*, and *Troodon*.

4 SOLNHOFEN, GERMANY

One of the exciting discoveries from this late Jurassic site was a partial skeleton of *Archeopteryx*, a rare feathered dinosaur. In 1860, a feather was found and, in 1861, a complete skeleton with feathers was uncovered. Many well-preserved fossils have come from Solnhofen, including 54 species of fishes and 28 kinds of reptiles. A complete dinosaur skeleton of *Compsognathus* has also been found.

5 GOBI DESERT, MONGOLIA

This late Cretaceous site in remote Mongolia was discovered by Dr Roy Chapman Andrews, of the American Museum of Natural History, in 1922. His expedition found the first dinosaur nest. The most famous find, however, was in 1971. This was the complete skeletons of two fighting dinosaurs—*Velociraptor* gripping the skull of *Protoceratops*. Other fossils from here include theropods, saruopods, and hadrosaurs.

6 LIAONING, CHINA

In 1996, a local farmer discovered a *Sinosaureoteryx* fossil at this early Cretaceous site. It was the first dinosaur specimen with primitive feathers. Two small dinosaurs with typical bird feathers, *Caudipteryx* and *Protoarcheopteryx*, were also found at this site, as were ancient bird skeletons. The fossils discovered at Liaoning show the many stages of evolution from small agile, running dinosaurs, to flying birds.

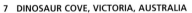

7 DINOSAUR COVE, VICTORIA, AUSTRALIA

In the 1980s, teams led by Tom Rich, of the Museum of Victoria, explored this site. Excavations involved using mining equipment to tunnel directly into sea cliffs. This was the first time that a dinosaur mine was created. Dinosaurs discovered here include *Atlascopscosaurus*, *Leaellynasaura*, and *Qantassaurus*—there are many other fossils waiting to be described. These dinosaurs lived in a polar forest.

8 VALLEY OF THE MOON, ARGENTINA

The Valley of the Moon and surrounding areas are famous for their late Triassic dinosaur fossils. The first fossils were found between 1959 and 1961. These include the oldest well-preserved dinosaur fossils in the world as well as more primitive reptiles that show evolutionary links to the first dinosaurs. The skeleton of the most primitive dinosaur, the tiny *Eoraptor*, was discovered here in 1988.

Hunting Dinosaurs

People have been finding dinosaur fossils for hundreds of years but it is only in the last 150 years that scientists realized that dinosaurs were different from other reptiles. It was not until 1858 that the first almost-complete dinosaur skeleton, a *Hadrosaurus,* was found. Fossil hunting increased in the 1870s, which led to many new dinosaur discoveries. Not all fossils are found by professional paleontologists. Fossil collecting is a popular hobby and some important specimens have been found by ordinary people with an interest in paleontology.

DINOSAUR HUNTERS OF THE PAST

GIDEON MANTELL
Mantell was a country doctor and amateur paleontologist during the 1800s. He spent much of his life studying dinosaurs, particularly *Iguanodon.*

SIR RICHARD OWEN
English paleontologist, Richard Owen, is known for making up the word "Dinosauria." He described hundreds of ancient animals, such as the Moa (right), and redescribed *Megalosaurus* (below).

Badlands are dry areas with little vegetation—the soil has been worn away by wind and rain. They are good places for dinosaur hunting because the bones are closer to the surface. Many fossils have been found in the badlands of the Rocky Mountains in the USA and Canada.

OTHNIEL CHARLES MARSH
Marsh (center, back row) was an American paleontologist in the 1800s. Marsh and his rival Edward Cope discovered more than 130 dinosaurs.

ROY CHAPMAN ANDREWS
Americans Andrews, a paleontologist, and Walter Granger, a geologist, made important dinosaur discoveries in China during the 1920s.

FAMOUS FINDS

AMAZING DISCOVERIES

The more fossils are found, the more information scientists can gain about dinosaurs. Every now and then someone finds a unique fossil that gives paleontologists new information. This can lead to a change in ideas about dinosaurs and their ancestors and to the naming of a new group of dinosaurs or a new anatomical feature. The three amazing specimens shown here are important for the information they give us about the development, behavior, and anatomy of dinosaurs.

SCIPIONYX
Scipionyx, "Skippy," is a baby dinosaur fossil from about 110 million years ago. The fine limestone has preserved parts of its liver, intestines, and muscles.

FIGHTING DINOSAURS IN THE GOBI DESERT
This famous fossil shows *Velociraptor* locked in a death grip with *Protoceratops*. A wall of sand collapsed on them, killing them instantly and preserving them intact.

FEATHERED FIND
This young *Microraptor* fossil was found in China. It is 130 million years old and is the first dinosaur fossil showing feathers growing on its hind limbs.

FINDING FOSSILS

Most fossils are found when a part of a skeleton has become exposed because surrounding rock has worn away. The best way to see fossils in the field is to walk around and look. Scientists carry a camera, water, notepad, pencil, and a map.

On a Dig

Paleontologists study maps and geology to find areas that could contain fossils. When they identify an area they mount an expedition to look for them. Once a fossil has been found, a map of the site is made. Each bone is labeled and photographed so the skeleton's position can be recreated after it is removed. When the bones are dug up, or excavated, they are encased in a jacket of plaster to keep them together and protect them on their journey to the museum. At the museum, the bones are carefully cleaned and laid in the position in which they were found. Scientists use microscopes, X-rays, and other technology to study the specimens. Damaged bones are hardened with glue and patched with special plastic. Rock and dirt samples are also taken and studied.

Dig it A lucky digger will run into another bone while uncovering the first.

Map it Photographs are taken every day to document each bone before it is removed.

Wrap it Fossils are wrapped in plaster, to prevent breakage, and labeled.

Move it Transporting fossils is risky. The bigger the fossil, the more care is needed.

IN THE FIELD

Field workers always dig or scrape from above the fossil, never from the side. Once a fossil is uncovered, it is vulnerable to wind and rain. Temperatures can reach as high as 122°F (50°C) in some sites. Water is essential for the plaster jackets that the bones are wrapped in and for the paleontologists to drink.

In the museum

In the museum, the process of "reverse excavation" begins. The bones are uncovered, hardened by glues, and repaired. They are photographed, measured, and documented. Each animal is given a catalogue number—a complete dinosaur could have more than 200 bones. If the fossil is a new species it is named according to the rules of the International Code of Zoological Nomenclature. The information gained from studying the fossil has to be published in a scientific journal before the name is official. If the dinosaur is going to be exhibited, a metal base is built to hold it up. A large dinosaur can take five years to exhibit and many hundreds of thousands of dollars. Museums hire scientists, artists, exhibitors, welders, collections specialists, writers, photographers, and computer specialists to help them. This is why museums sometimes ask for donations of money.

The Smithsonian Institution in Washington, DC, USA, is scheduled to get a new dinosaur hall in 2014. The Carnegie Museum in Pittsburgh, USA, opened its new dinosaur hall in 2008.

Paleontologists are the second biggest buyers of dental picks! These fine tools are essential for detailed work.

Specimens are laid out in "life position" so the staff can tell how much space is needed to mount the whole skeleton.

THE FINAL TOUCH

Welding the iron base for an exhibit is difficult. Each piece of metal is matched exactly with each fossil bone. Supports are placed between the iron and the fossil to absorb knocks. This is the best way to make dinosaurs "live again."

Reconstructing Dinosaurs

Many dinosaur bones, such as thighbones and jaws, have shapes that are easily recognized. Scientists can guess at how other bones fit together by looking at the way they were found and by studying other dinosaurs and living reptiles. In the same way, they can guess at the shape of missing bones. Missing parts are made from plastics, fiberglass, or plaster and fitted into place. Scientists can tell a lot about dinosaur muscles by studying birds and crocodiles. They can see how muscles attached to the skeleton by studying the scars that muscles left on the bones. When it comes to the skin, there are good examples of preserved skin patterns from dinosaurs, which give us clues to the pattern and texture of the skin. Color, however, is an artist's choice.

BODY BUILDING

The reconstruction of *Baryonyx*, "heavy claw," a 30-foot (9-m) early Cretaceous theropod, began with the discovery of a single claw. Paleontologists from all over the world cooperated to find the rest of the bones and restore it to its former glory.

Missing links For mounted skeletons, missing parts are sculpted from plastics, fiberglass, and plaster.

Drawings Scientific illustrators use a dotting, or stippling, technique to show the fine shading on bones.

LEARNING FROM LIVING CREATURES

Birds and crocodiles teach us many things about their extinct relatives—including body structure and eating habits. A dinosaur's skeleton has features in common with crocodile and bird skeletons. Scientists compare bones of dinosaurs with those of crocodiles to see what changes were made to enable the dinosaur's upright stance.

They also compare theropod skeletons with those of birds to see what had to change to allow birds to fly. The next time you go to a museum, look at the backbones that attach to the hip in a crocodile, dinosaur, and bird. You should see an increasing number of bones fused together.

Baryonyx's skin was recreated by studying the pattern and texture of the skin of reptiles, such as snakes.

Baryonyx's lower jaw was curved like that of a fish-eating crocodile. It probably used its claws to "hook" fish.

Birds have three toes pointing forward and a fourth pointing backward—the same as meat-eating dinosaurs.

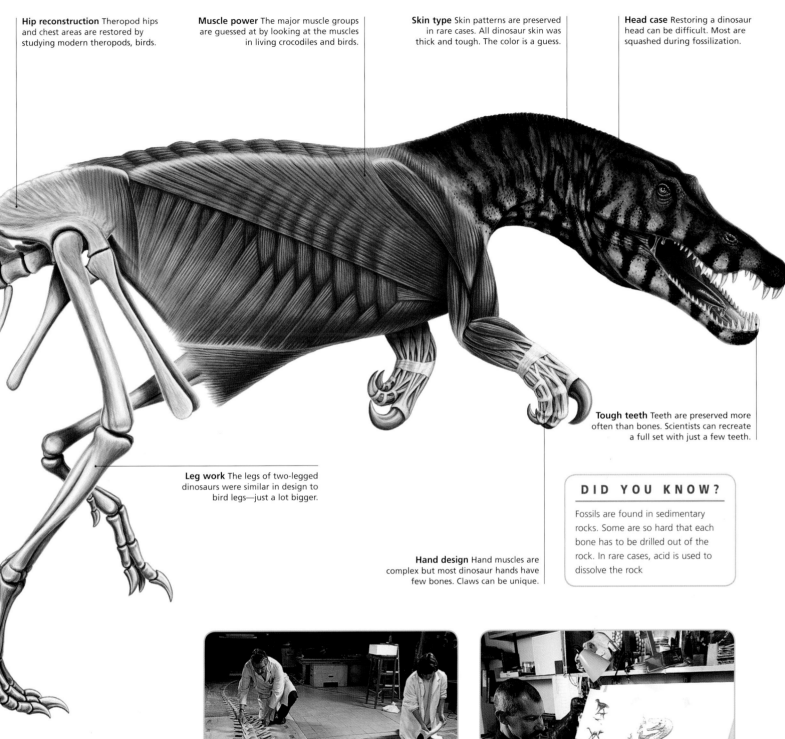

Hip reconstruction Theropod hips and chest areas are restored by studying modern theropods, birds.

Muscle power The major muscle groups are guessed at by looking at the muscles in living crocodiles and birds.

Skin type Skin patterns are preserved in rare cases. All dinosaur skin was thick and tough. The color is a guess.

Head case Restoring a dinosaur head can be difficult. Most are squashed during fossilization.

Tough teeth Teeth are preserved more often than bones. Scientists can recreate a full set with just a few teeth.

Leg work The legs of two-legged dinosaurs were similar in design to bird legs—just a lot bigger.

Hand design Hand muscles are complex but most dinosaur hands have few bones. Claws can be unique.

DID YOU KNOW?

Fossils are found in sedimentary rocks. Some are so hard that each bone has to be drilled out of the rock. In rare cases, acid is used to dissolve the rock

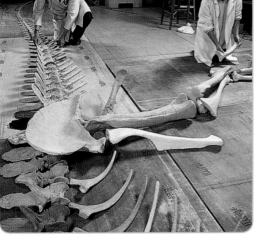

Paleontologists lay out the entire skeleton after it has been prepared and conserved. In this way they can see what bones are missing. By looking at similar bones in other, closely related dinosaurs, they can guess at the shapes of the missing bones.

Scientific illustrators make accurate drawings of fossils. Artists work with paleontologists to make sure the dinosaur's posture is correct. Mesozoic plant experts and geologists also work with artists to help describe the dinosaur's environment.

Myths and Legends

Myths and legends about dinosaurs have been around for centuries. It is easy to imagine how puzzling, and frightening, it would have been for the first people who found these enormous bones. Even though dinosaurs died out 61 million years before humans appeared on Earth, we continue to be fascinated by these huge, ancient animals. The earliest known description of a dinosaur came from China, almost 3,000 years ago—they thought they were fossils of the mythological animal, the dragon. In England, 300 years ago, the thighbone of a *Megalosaurus* was mistaken for a bone from a huge elephant—then it was thought to be from a giant human. In 1820, dinosaur tracks were believed to be the footprints of prehistoric birds.

DID YOU KNOW?

The ancient Chinese ground up dinosaur fossils, known as "dragon bones" and "dragon teeth," to use in special medicines and magic powders. Today some traditional Chinese medicine contains small amounts of powdered bones and teeth from dinosaur fossils.

Byronosaurus It is easy to imagine how bones from this *Byronosaurus* could be mistaken for the bones of a dragon.

DRAGONS AND DINOSAURS

When Chinese scholars first discovered dinosaur fossils they thought they were the bones of powerful dragons, which have been a part of Chinese mythology for thousands of years.

CHANGING IDEAS

IGUANODON

In 1825, *Iguanodon* became the second dinosaur to be scientifically named. How its bones have been interpreted since then shows us how much scientists have progressed and how much our ideas of what dinosaurs looked like have changed.

Dragon In one magazine restoration from the 1880s, *Iguanodon* ended up looking like a dragon.

Reptile The most common restoration of *Iguanodon* during the 1890s looked like a two-legged reptile with its tail dragging on the ground.

Iguana Scientists first thought *Iguanodon* was a giant iguana because its teeth resembled those of an iguana.

Iguanodon The modern reconstruction, based on its skeleton, muscles, and ligaments, shows *Iguanodon* on all fours with its tail held high. The single most important change is that the nose horn on the 1825 original reconstruction is now known to be a thumb spike.

A–Z of Dinosaurs

Abelisaurus

PRONUNCIATION: ah-BEL-ee-SAW-rus

This dinosaur from South America is part of a group of meat eaters that evolved separately from the more famous tyrannosaurs on the northern continents. It had a high skull and extremely powerful jaw muscles—its jaw could slam shut so fast that its prey did not have time to react. Scientists have found a 3-feet (1-m) long skull but they do not know how large *Abelisaurus* grew.

THE FACTS

MEANING: After Roberto Abel

DATE: Late Cretaceous

GROUP: Theropoda

DIET: Meat

SIZE: 6.6 feet (2 m) long

FOSSIL LOCATIONS: Argentina 1985

Abelisaurus

Agustinia

PRONUNCIATION: ah-goo-STEE-nee-a

This sauropod looked like a combination stegosaur, ankylosaur, and porcupine. Its skin was covered with armor-like bony lumps, called osteoderms. Its back was covered with two rows of spikes that stuck out sideways. Some spikes were up to 29 inches (75 cm) long. It also had spikes on its tail and possibly on its neck. *Agustinia* is only known from parts of skeletons. Discoveries of new fossils may lead scientists to believe it looked even more strange than we think today.

THE FACTS

MEANING: After Agustin Martinelli

DATE: Early Cretaceous

GROUP: Sauropodamorpha

DIET: Plants

SIZE: 50 feet (15 m) long

FOSSIL LOCATIONS: Argentina 1999

Agustinia

Albertoceratops

THE FACTS

MEANING: Alberta (Canada) horned face
DATE: Late Cretaceous
GROUP: Theropoda
DIET: Plants
SIZE: 16 feet (5 m) long
FOSSIL LOCATIONS: USA, Canada 2007

PRONUNCIATION: al-BER-to-SER-a-tops

This horned dinosaur looked as if it had a set of can-openers at the back of its head, behind its frill. These horns protected its frill from being bitten by tyrannosaurs that lived at the same time. Shaking its head from side to side would have moved these spikes like small pickaxes. Its face was protected by two long brow horns, which was unusual for this type of dinosaur. *Albertoceratops* was one of the centrosaurines, a group of dinosaurs that had a single large horn over their nose.

Albertoceratops

Albertosaurus

PRONUNCIATION: al-BER-to-SAW-rus

This dinosaur was built just like its closest relative, *Tyrannosaurus rex,* but was not as powerful or as tall. The two dinosaurs looked almost identical, specially to terrified plant eaters, such as duckbills and horned dinosaurs. *Albertosaurus* had one row of teeth in each jaw but had at least one row of replacement teeth ready to come through. It had tiny, two-fingered hands and its arms were too short to put food to its mouth—scientists are not sure what they were used for.

THE FACTS

MEANING: Alberta (Canada) lizard
DATE: Late Cretaceous
GROUP: Theropoda
DIET: Meat
SIZE: 26 feet (8 m) long
FOSSIL LOCATIONS: USA, Canada 1905

Albertosaurus

Allosaurus

PRONUNCIATION: AL-oh-SAW-rus

This is one of the most well-known dinosaurs. It has become the defining Jurassic meat eater and the model of a carnosaur—a large, heavily built theropod. *Allosaurus* was terrifying at any stage of its life. As a baby it ate lizards, mammals, and insects. As a kid it ate other baby dinosaurs. As a teenager it ate anything smaller than itself. As an adult it ate everything—what it could not hunt it scavenged. Its arms were muscular and its serrated teeth ripped flesh faster than a chainsaw.

THE FACTS

MEANING:	Other lizard
DATE:	Late Jurassic
GROUP:	Theropoda
DIET:	Meat
SIZE:	39 feet (12 m) long
FOSSIL LOCATIONS:	USA 1877

Allosaurus

Massive hind limbs supported *Allosaurus*'s weight but they were also built for speed.

ALLOSAURUS ANATOMY

Allosaurus was well equipped for hunting. Strong, grasping claws on its front legs, razor-sharp teeth, and a flexible jaw made this dinosaur a formidable predator.

Claws   Eye | Teeth | Nostril

Sharp claws
Three-fingered hands ended in hooked claws. It may have used them like grappling hooks.

Flexible jaws
A flexible joint in its lower jaw allowed its jaw to bend outward and enlarge its mouth for a deadlier bite.

Flexible joint

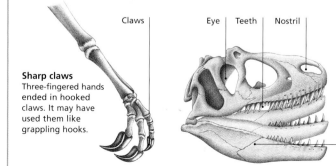

FEEDING THE FAMILY

Allosaurus roamed the forests of North America 150 million years ago. It hunted mostly small plant eaters, such as *Camptosaurus,* and sometimes, giant sauropods, such as *Diplodocus*. These dinosaurs often hunted in pairs or packs but they also hunted on their own.

Alvarezsaurus

PRONUNCIATION: ahl-vahr-ez-SAW-rus

This rare dinosaur was close to the group of meat eaters that was most related to birds. Although it was from South America, it had features similar to those of the ornithomimids, or ostrich-like dinosaurs, of North America. Not much is known about this dinosaur because scientists lack a complete skeleton, but we know it could outrun most other dinosaurs and could catch small prey.

THE FACTS

MEANING: After Don Gregorio Alvarez
DATE: Late Cretaceous
GROUP: Theropoda
DIET: Meat
SIZE: 6 feet (2 m) long
FOSSIL LOCATIONS: Argentina 1991

Alvarezsaurus

Alwalkeria

PRONUNCIATION: al-wah-KEER-ee-a

This unusual dinosaur from India may have eaten both plants and meat. Its teeth were unlike those of most other dinosaurs—some were straight and others were curved. The most complete skull fossil found is small. This could mean the dinosaur was a baby and scientists have yet to find an adult. If it was an adult, this dinosaur would have been small enough to sit in your lap.

THE FACTS

MEANING: After Alick Walker
DATE: Late Triassic
GROUP: Sauropodamorpha
DIET: Plants and meat
SIZE: 3 feet (1 m) long
FOSSIL LOCATIONS: India 1986

DID YOU KNOW?

Omnivores eat both meat and plants. Few dinosaurs were omnivores and, while they ate both plants and animals, meat was the main part of their diet. Omnivores usually ate whatever they could find, such as berries and seeds, or grubs and insects.

Alwalkeria

THE FACTS

MEANING: From La Amarga (Argentina)

DATE: Early Cretaceous

GROUP: Sauropodamorpha

DIET: Plants

SIZE: 32 feet (10 m) long

FOSSIL LOCATIONS: Argentina 1991

Amargasaurus

PRONUNCIATION: ah-MAHR-goh-SAW-rus

At only 32 feet (10 m) long, this dinosaur was small for a sauropod, or "long-neck." It had one other feature that set it apart from other sauropods: two parallel rows of tall spines that ran down its neck and back. Scientists have different ideas about what these tall "sails" were used for—they may have been used for self-defense.

Amargasaurus

Anchisaurus footprints were found in Connecticut sandstone in 1865.

Anchisaurus

Anchisaurus

PRONUNCIATION: ANG-ki-SAW-rus

As one of the smaller and earliest sauropods, *Anchisaurus* is not as famous as the Jurassic giants. It weighed 77 pounds (35 kg) and could eat only ground-level plants. It had a thumb claw and blunt teeth. It was a slow walker and could not outrun the meat eaters of its day. This dinosaur was named in 1885, well after its fossil footprints were discovered.

THE FACTS

MEANING: Similar lizard

DATE: Early Jurassic

GROUP: Sauropodamorpha

DIET: Plants

SIZE: 8 feet (2.4 m) long

FOSSIL LOCATIONS: USA 1885

Ankylosaurus

PRONUNCIATION: an-KEE-loh-SAW-rus

The outside of *Ankylosaurus*'s skull was covered with armor—just imagine having a bone helmet fused to your skull! The nose passage had up to eight chambers, which may have been used for temperature control or for increasing its sense of smell. Its back had flexible armor plating and the end of its tail had a massive bone club. When it swung its tail from side to side, it was at just the right height to smash a tyrannosaur's knee. It could not outrun a meat eater but it was a heavy, movable fort that could not be flipped over.

THE FACTS

MEANING: Fused lizard

DATE: Late Cretaceous

GROUP: Ankylosauria

DIET: Plants

SIZE: 33 feet (10 m) long

FOSSIL LOCATIONS: USA, Canada 2006

 Ankylosaurus

This fossil was discovered in the Gobi Desert. *Ankylosaurus* had an armor of bone that was fused together to protect its body.

The heavy tail club was used like a wrecking ball and could seriously damage an attacking predator.

TOUGH SKIN

Ankylosaurus wore a suit of armor that consisted of thick, bony plates and spikes along its back.

THE FACTS

MEANING: Antarctic shield

DATE: Late Cretaceous

GROUP: Ankylosauria

DIET: Plants

SIZE: 13 feet (4 m) long

FOSSIL LOCATIONS: Antarctica 2006

Antarctopelta

PRONUNCIATION: ANT-ark-toe-PELL-ta

Antarctopelta had a body shield and many spikes. Scientists do not know if it had a club at the end of its tail. *Antarctopelta* had similarities to earlier ankylosaurs but it appeared much later. This led scientists to believe that it became isolated from other ankylosaurs that continued to evolve on the main continents.

Antarctopelta

THE FACTS

MEANING: Deceptive lizard

DATE: Late Jurassic

GROUP: Sauropodamorpha

DIET: Plants

SIZE: 82 feet (25 m) long

FOSSIL LOCATIONS: USA 1877

Apatosaurus

PRONUNCIATION: a-PAT-o-SAW-rus

Once known as *Brontosaurus*, this mulching machine had a massive body. It had teeth that were like the prongs on a rake—it could strip plant matter from trees but not chew it. Although it had only one thumb claw on its front feet, the claw had enough force behind it to rip a meat eater in two. Once it grew to full adult size, a healthy *Apatosaurus* was safe from almost all predators.

Apatosaurus

Argentinosaurus

PRONUNCIATION: ah-jen-TEEN-oh-SAW-rus

Some scientists believe that *Argentinosaurus* was the largest animal to walk on Earth. Although only a few bones have been found, they include huge vertebrae up to 4 feet (1.2 m) high. This dinosaur weighed more than 70 tons and grew to a massive 70 feet (21.4 m) tall—it could look in the window of the fifth floor of a building. It was found in the Patagonia region of Argentina where other giant dinosaurs have been found, including *Giganotosaurus*.

DID YOU KNOW?

There are several dinosaurs that could have been the biggest. The leader, so far, is *Amphicoelias* at 197 feet (60 m)—but this dinosaur's description of is based only on drawings of a lost fossil!

□ *Argentinosaurus*

THE FACTS

MEANING: Argentina lizard

DATE: Late Cretaceous

GROUP: Sauropodamorpha

DIET: Plants

SIZE: 149 feet (48 m) long

FOSSIL LOCATIONS: Argentina 1993

Atlascopcosaurus

PRONUNCIATION: AT-las-KOP-koh-SAW-rus

At 10 feet (3 m) long, this small, agile plant eater spent its life eating leaves and trying not to be spotted by faster meat eaters. It may have lived in family groups or small herds. Dinosaur Cove, Victoria, Australia, where *Atlascopcosaurus* fossils were found, is probably more famous than a lot of the dinosaurs that were found there. Dinosaur Cove had to be excavated by drilling directly into sea cliffs with mining equipment—this was the first dinosaur mine. *Atlascopcosaurus* was named for the company that supplied the equipment for the excavation.

Atlascopcosaurus

THE FACTS

MEANING: Atlas Corporation lizard

DATE: Early Cretaceous

GROUP: Ornithopoda

DIET: Plants

SIZE: 10 feet (3 m) long

FOSSIL LOCATIONS: Australia 1989

Avimimus

PRONUNCIATION: AY-vee-MY-mus

THE FACTS

MEANING: Bird mimic

DATE: Late Cretaceous

GROUP: Theropoda

DIET: Meat

SIZE: 5 feet (1.5 m) long

FOSSIL LOCATIONS: Mongolia 1981

Avimimus

This lightly built, birdlike dinosaur was a type of *Oviraptor*. It was a predator that lived in semi-arid conditions and may have eaten both plants and animals. It had long legs, a long neck, and a beak but no teeth. Scientists think it was fully feathered but it probably could not fly. *Avimimus* is one of the fastest dinosaurs known.

Avimimus had a long neck and short head with a toothless mouth. Instead of teeth it had a powerful and sharp beak.

Bambiraptor

PRONUNCIATION: BAM-bee-RAP-tor

What we know about this dinosaur is based on one fossil that was found about 95 percent complete. From this one specimen scientists could tell it was young, had a relatively large brain, and its forearms could have folded against its body in the way a bird's can. It belonged to a group of feathered dinosaurs—though the fossil had no feathers preserved with it. *Bambiraptor* could be the fossil of another birdlike dinosaur, *Saurornitholestes,* but scientists will not know until more fossils can be studied.

THE FACTS

MEANING: Bambi thief

DATE: Late Cretaceous

GROUP: Theropoda

DIET: Meat

SIZE: 5 feet (1.5 m) long

FOSSIL LOCATIONS: USA 2000

Bambiraptor

Barosaurus

PRONUNCIATION: BAH-roh-SAW-rus

This Jurassic giant has been described as "*Diplodocus*–only longer." It is one of the rarest members of the family Diplodocidae. *Barosaurus*'s head was small and so were its teeth. It ate soft plant material, unlike another dinosaur that lived at the same time, *Camarasaurus,* which ate tougher, more fibrous plants. Therefore, even though *Barosaurus* and *Camarasaurus* lived side by side, they did not compete with each other for food.

THE FACTS

MEANING: Heavy lizard

DATE: Late Jurassic

GROUP: Sauropodamorpha

DIET: Plants

SIZE: 80 feet (26 m) long

FOSSIL LOCATIONS: USA 1890

Barosaurus

Baryonx had 64 teeth. This was more than most theropods had. Its teeth were not as flat as those of other theropods and were finely serrated.

Baryonyx

PRONUNCIATION: BARE-ee-ON-iks

This dinosaur lived along the shorelines and hunted in the water for fish. It had a long, slender neck and a skull shaped like a crocodile's. It probably used its slender snout to snap prey out of the water in the same way crocodiles do today. It would have been a better hunter than bears or crocodiles.

Baryonyx

THE FACTS

MEANING:	Heavy claw
DATE:	Early Cretaceous
GROUP:	Theropoda
DIET:	Meat
SIZE:	30 feet (9 m) long
FOSSIL LOCATIONS:	England 1986

BARYONYX HANDS

The first part of *Baryonyx* to be discovered was its huge claw, which was about 14 inches (35 cm) long.

Baryonyx had powerful arms and large hands. It used its hands to hook prey.

FISH EATER

Baryonyx's thin jaw and finely serrated teeth led scientists to believe it was not capable of attacking and bringing down large animals. It was probably a fish eater.

Beipiaosaurus

PRONUNCIATION: bay-peow-SAW-rus

This dinosaur belonged to the oddest group of dinosaurs, the therizinosaurs. Therizinosaurs were birdlike dinosaurs with long necks, small heads, and teeth that seemed more suited to eating plants. *Beipiaosaurus* was the size of a football player, in height and weight. Its body was covered with feathers but it could not fly. Some of its bones were fused together to form a structure that birds today use to help them fly—we do not know why *Beipiaosaurus* had this bone structure.

THE FACTS

MEANING: Lizard from Beipiao, China

DATE: Late Cretaceous

GROUP: Theropoda

DIET: Meat

SIZE: 7.3 feet (2.2 m) long

FOSSIL LOCATIONS: China 1999

Beipiaosaurus

Bonitasaura

PRONUNCIATION: bo-NEE-ta -SAW-ruh

Bonitasaura was a huge plant eater with a wide mouth that looked a little like the front of a straight-edged shovel. It had lots of small teeth like the prongs on a rake, which strained its food. Behind its teeth was a beaklike structure that cut off the plant material. Its muscular neck helped it rip leaves and small branches from trees.

THE FACTS

MEANING: Lizard from the La Bonita quarry

DATE: Late Cretaceous

GROUP: Sauropodamorpha

DIET: Plants

SIZE: 30 feet (9 m) long

FOSSIL LOCATIONS: Argentina 2004

Bonitasaura

Brachiosaurus

PRONUNCIATION: BRAK-ee-oh-SAW-rus

If this giant lived today, it could look into the window of a five-story building—it would have taken more than 30 years to grow this high. It is one of the few dinosaurs with front arms longer than its legs. An adult *Brachiosaurus* stood in the same way a giraffe does—both animals fed on leaves from the treetops.

Brachiosaurus

THE FACTS

MEANING:	Arm lizard
DATE:	Late Jurassic
GROUP:	Sauropodamorpha
DIET:	Plants
SIZE:	82 feet (25 m) long
FOSSIL LOCATIONS:	USA, Tanzania 1903

Byronosaurus

PRONUNCIATION: BY-ron-o-SAW-rus

This agile meat eater could only attack small animals because it was slight. It weighed only 11 pounds (5 kg) and was about 17 inches (43 cm) high. Its small, thin teeth were unlike the thick sawlike teeth of its relatives, the troodontids. This limited *Byronosaurus*'s diet to soft-bodied animals, such as birds, small mammals, insects, and frogs. Its snout was long, like a wolfhound's, which helped protect its eyes during a fight.

THE FACTS

MEANING:	Byron's lizard (after Byron Jaffe)
DATE:	Late Cretaceous
GROUP:	Ornithopoda
DIET:	Plants
SIZE:	5 feet (1.5 m) long
FOSSIL LOCATIONS:	Mongolia 2000

Byronosaurus

Camarasaurus

PRONUNCIATION: KAM-a-ra-SAW-rus

This is the most common sauropod from the late Jurassic of the western United States. It is known from many complete skeletons from every age group and is one of the best known of all the dinosaurs. It was a large plant eater that specialized in eating hard, fibrous vegetation. Its teeth were 6 inches (16 cm) long and were designed to strip branches off trees. It had an expanded nose cavity, which could mean it had an excellent sense of smell. It probably traveled in herds.

Camarasaurus had spoon-shaped cutting teeth but no grinding teeth. However, it could reach high into trees to tear away leaves.

THE FACTS
MEANING:	Chambered lizard
DATE:	Late Jurassic
GROUP:	Sauropodamorpha
DIET:	Plants
SIZE:	59 feet (18 m) long
FOSSIL LOCATIONS:	USA 1877

Camarasaurus

Carcharadontosaurus

PRONUNCIATION: kuh-KAR-oh-dont-oh-SAW-rus

This meat eater lived in Africa about 90 million years ago. It was once thought to have been the same size as *Tyrannosaurus rex* but scientists now know it was smaller. Its skull was not as heavy as *T. rex*'s but its bite was faster and its teeth were sharper and better designed for cutting. *Carcharodontosaurus* probably hunted sauropods more than any other plant eater. Its teeth were triangular and did not curve back as much as those of other theropods—they were sharklike, which explains its name.

THE FACTS
MEANING:	Shark-tooth lizard
DATE:	Early Cretaceous
GROUP:	Theropoda
DIET:	Meat
SIZE:	43 feet (13 m) long
FOSSIL LOCATIONS:	North Africa 1931

Carcharadontosaurus

Carnotaurus

Carnotaurus

PRONUNCIATION: KAR-noh-TAW-rus

This small, slightly built meat eater was one of the abelisaurs, a group of theropods common in the southern continents. It had two outstanding features: the horns above its eyes and its unusual forearms. It had a narrow skull and it may have been an ambush predator that hunted larger planting-eating dinosaurs and small dinosaurs. Its skull was too fragile for combat so it was probably only used for breaking up dead dinosaurs.

THE FACTS

MEANING: Meat (eating) bull

DATE: Early Cretaceous

GROUP: Theropoda

DIET: Meat

SIZE: 6 feet (8 m) long

FOSSIL LOCATIONS: Argentina 1985

Caudipteryx

Caudipteryx

PRONUNCIATION: kaw-DIP-ter-iks

When this fossil was found it created a sensation. This was a dinosaur that had fully evolved feathers all over its body. Although it could not fly, but possibly glided, the feathers proved that dinosaurs and birds formed a single group. *Caudipteryx* also had stomach stones, called gastroliths, which means it probably ate plants and animals—the gastroliths were used to crushed the plants.

THE FACTS

MEANING: Tail feather

DATE: Early Cretaceous

GROUP: Theropoda

DIET: Plants and meat

SIZE: 3 feet (1 m) long

FOSSIL LOCATIONS: China 1998

Centrosaurus

PRONUNCIATION: SEN-tro-SAW-rus

This horned ornithischian has its own World Heritage Park: Dinosaur Provincial Park in Alberta, Canada. The park contains a site with tens of thousands *Centrosaurus* skeletons. Scientists think a herd of these dinosaurs tried to cross a flooding river, and many drowned. There are more unexcavated skeletons of *Centrosaurus* than there are dinosaur paleontologists in the world.

Centrosaurus

THE FACTS

MEANING:	Pointed horn lizard
DATE:	Late Cretaceous
GROUP:	Ceratopsia
DIET:	Plants
SIZE:	20 feet (6 m) long
FOSSIL LOCATIONS:	Canada 1904

Ceratosaurus

PRONUNCIATION: se-RAT-o-SAW-rus

Ceratosaurus is a meat-eating dinosaur that lived at the end of the Jurassic. It belonged to a group of early theropods. Its main feature was the horn on the end of its nose, which only appeared on fully grown adults. The horn was too small to be used actively for defense so it was probably used to display threat. Only one complete skull and skeleton of this dinosaur has ever been found.

THE FACTS

MEANING:	Horned lizard
DATE:	Late Jurassic
GROUP:	Theropoda
DIET:	Meat
SIZE:	20 feet (6 m) long
FOSSIL LOCATIONS:	USA 1884

Ceratosaurus

Chasmosaurus

PRONUNCIATION: KAS-mo-SAW-rus

Chasmosaurus belongs to the group of dinosaurs that includes *Triceratops*. The brow horns over its eye and nose area were long. The frill was also long because it had to counterbalance the face where the jaw muscles began—and it made a good threatening display. So many different looking skulls have been found that many *Chasmosaurus* species were named. However, these differences were probably due to health, age, environment, and gender.

THE FACTS

MEANING:	Opening-hollow lizard
DATE:	Late Cretaceous
GROUP:	Ceratopsia
DIET:	Plants
SIZE:	17 feet (5 m) long
FOSSIL LOCATIONS:	USA, Canada 1914

HERBIVORE HERDS

Plant-eating dinosaurs often traveled in herds in search of food. *Chasmosaurus* is seen here with another North American dinosaur, the crested *Corythosaurus*. Each herd had more than 1,000 dinosaurs.

☐ *Chasmosaurus*

Coelophysis

PRONUNCIATION: SEE-lo-FY-sis

This Triassic theropod is known from many skeletons from, New Mexico, USA. Its snout was long and so were its arms, which means it could easily have captured small prey. During the time it lived, *Coelophysis* was one of the fastest animals on Earth. Several skeletons have been found with young *Coelophysis* in the area where the stomach would have been. This means that these dinosaurs died before they could digest their last supper.

The long head and neck of *Coelophysis* is clearly seen in attack positions.

THE FACTS

MEANING: Hollow form

DATE: Late Triassic

GROUP: Theropoda

DIET: Meat

SIZE: 10 feet (3 m) long

FOSSIL LOCATIONS: USA 1889

Coelophysis

Compsognathus

PRONUNCIATION: KOMP-sog-NA-thus

Compsognathus was a theropod the size of a large turkey, and an active predator of small animals. One specimen has a complete lizard inside its stomach—it had been swallowed whole. Its relatively small teeth were adapted to grabbing prey but not to slicing them, as bigger theropods' teeth were. *Compsognathus* was found in the same fossil deposit as the first bird, *Archeopteryx*, and the famous pterosaurs *Rhamphorhynchus* and *Pterodactylus*. They all lived in a lagoon-like area.

Compsognathus was an agile predator. It may also have been two-fingered but the hands found were not intact so scientists cannot be sure.

THE FACTS

MEANING: Elegant jaw

DATE: Late Jurassic

GROUP: Theropoda

DIET: Meat

SIZE: 3 feet (1 m) long

FOSSIL LOCATIONS: France, Germany 1859

Compsognathus

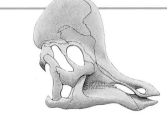

This skull shows the height of the crest. Large-crested individuals are thought to have been adult males. They may have used their crests to attract females and to intimidate other males.

Corythosaurus

PRONUNCIATION: ko-RITH-o-SAW-rus

This crested duckbill dinosaur appears in most books on dinosaurs. Its crest, or "helmet," had two hollow chambers that probably helped control humidity and improved its sense of smell. It was also important in making noises. The shape of its skull and the sounds it made have been compared to that of a French horn. The crest was made mostly of upper-lip bone, which grew back over the top of its skull.

Corythosaurus

THE FACTS
MEANING: (Corinthian) helmet lizard

DATE: Late Cretaceous

GROUP: Ornithopoda

DIET: Plants

SIZE: 33 feet (10 m) long

FOSSIL LOCATIONS: Canada 1914

Cyrolophosaurus

PRONUNCIATION: KYR-oh-loh-foh-SAW-rus

This dinosaur's nickname is "Elvis" because of the elaborate, comblike crest on its skull. The crest was too fragile to be protective but, if it was colored, it would have made a good display during mating season. This early Jurassic theropod was discovered 398 miles (640 km) from the South Pole, at about 13,000 feet (4,000 m) above sea level. Paleontologists and geologists risked their lives in extreme conditions to collect these bones.

Cyrolophosaurus

THE FACTS
MEANING: Cold crested lizard

DATE: Early Jurassic

GROUP: Theropoda

DIET: Meat

SIZE: 24 feet (7.5 m) long

FOSSIL LOCATIONS: Antarctica 1994

Dacentrurus

PRONUNCIATION: da-sen-TROO-rus

This gigantic, European stegosaur lived
at the same time as *Stegosaurus.* Both
dinosaurs had long spikes and plates along
their backs. *Dacentrurus*'s legs were pillar-
like and its thighbone was much longer
than its shinbone. It was unable to outrun
a theropod but it had a great defense—its
tail was designed to swing from side to side,
and the spikes were long enough to go right
through a theropod's leg.

THE FACTS

MEANING:	Very sharp tail
DATE:	Late Jurassic
GROUP:	Stegosauria
DIET:	Plants
SIZE:	26 feet (8 m) long
FOSSIL LOCATIONS:	England 1902

Dacentrurus

DEINONYCHUS ANATOMY

What *Deinonychus* lacked in size, it made up for in claw. Its claw could first stab, then swivel, fatally wounding its prey. Its claws and sharp teeth made it a fierce predator.

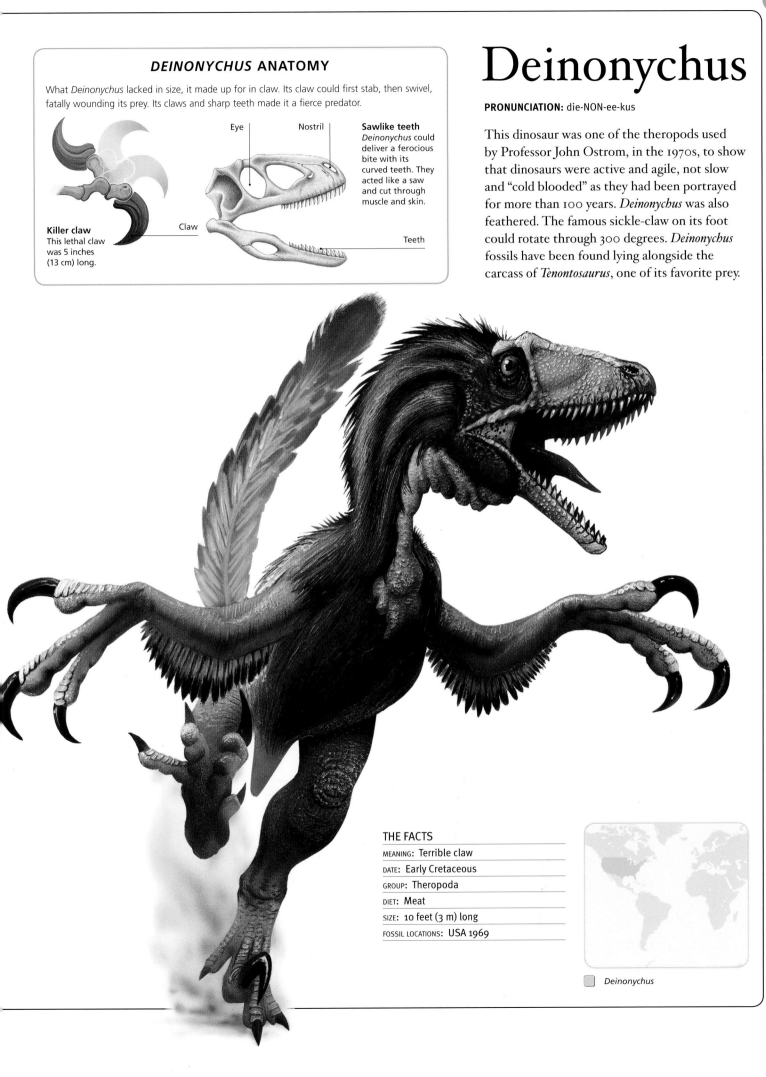

Killer claw
This lethal claw was 5 inches (13 cm) long.

Claw

Eye

Nostril

Sawlike teeth
Deinonychus could deliver a ferocious bite with its curved teeth. They acted like a saw and cut through muscle and skin.

Teeth

Deinonychus

PRONUNCIATION: die-NON-ee-kus

This dinosaur was one of the theropods used by Professor John Ostrom, in the 1970s, to show that dinosaurs were active and agile, not slow and "cold blooded" as they had been portrayed for more than 100 years. *Deinonychus* was also feathered. The famous sickle-claw on its foot could rotate through 300 degrees. *Deinonychus* fossils have been found lying alongside the carcass of *Tenontosaurus*, one of its favorite prey.

THE FACTS

MEANING: **Terrible claw**
DATE: **Early Cretaceous**
GROUP: **Theropoda**
DIET: **Meat**
SIZE: **10 feet (3 m) long**
FOSSIL LOCATIONS: **USA 1969**

Deinonychus

Dilong

PRONUNCIATION: dee-LONG

Dilong was a feathered dinosaur from the famous Yixian Formation in China. Many feathered dinosaurs have been found here and fossil preservation is better than in most places in the world. *Dilong* had body feathers, not flight feathers, and it was a ground runner. Its skeleton has many features in common with tyrannosaurs and it may have been an early member of the line that led to *Tyrannosaurus rex*.

THE FACTS

MEANING: Emperor dragon

DATE: Early Cretaceous

GROUP: Theropoda

DIET: Meat

SIZE: 6.5 feet (2 m) long

FOSSIL LOCATIONS: China 2004

Dilong

Dilophosaurus

PRONUNCIATION: die-LOF-o-SAW-rus

This early Jurassic theropod was not as tall as *Allosaurus* but it was faster than most animals alive at the time. Its name comes from the two large crests on top of its head. The bones that made up these crests were paper-thin and light would have passed through them if they were held up to the sun. They were probably used for display only.

THE FACTS

MEANING: Two-crested lizard

DATE: Early Jurassic

GROUP: Theropoda

DIET: Meat

SIZE: 20 feet (6 m) long

FOSSIL LOCATIONS: China, USA 1970

Dilophosaurus

This skull shows the crest on the head. It may have been a device that helped dinosaurs distinguish one species from another.

DIPLODOCUS FOOT

Diplodocus had four big feet to help carry its large weight. It also walked on its toes, as elephants do.

Toes

Diplodocus

Diplodocus

PRONUNCIATION: dip-LOD-o-kus

If the word "sleek" could be applied to a sauropod, then that would describe *Diplodocus*. Its main body was slightly larger than that of an elephant. Its great length came from its long neck and tail. *Diplodocus* stood on the edge of a river or lake and used its neck like a vacuum cleaner. Its pencil-like teeth raked up soft-fiber plants. Its food was swallowed whole—sauropods could not chew.

THE FACTS

MEANING: Double-beam

DATE: Late Jurassic

GROUP: Sauropodamorpha

DIET: Plants

SIZE: 98 feet (30 m) long

FOSSIL LOCATIONS: USA 1878

BIG REACH

Diplodocus's back legs were longer than its front legs. It probably reared up onto its hind legs to reach leaves in taller trees or perhaps to scare off predators.

Dracorex

PRONUNCIATION: DRAK-o-reks

The full name of this dinosaur is *Dracorex hogwartsia*, which means "dragon-king of Hogwart's School of Witchcraft and Wizardry." Its description is based on a single specimen. In 2007, a new study led several scientists to believe that *Dracorex* was a young *Pachycephalosaurus* and that another dinosaur, *Stygimoloch,* was an young adult. This is like saying that *Dracorex* was the young teenager, *Stygimoloch* was the late teenager, and *Pachycephalosaurus* was the adult.

THE FACTS

MEANING:	Dragon king
DATE:	Late Cretaceous
GROUP:	Pachycephalosauria
DIET:	Plants
SIZE:	10 feet (3 m) long
FOSSIL LOCATIONS:	USA 2006

Dracorex

Dromaeosaurus

PRONUNCIATION: DROH-mee-o-SAW-rus

This small theropod was more heavily built than the other members of its family. Its teeth were thick enough to be used for tearing but not slicing. Its arms featured ornamental feathers but it could not fly. This dinosaur has sometimes been called "the wolf of the Cretaceous." This is misleading because it had few attributes of a wolf—it was a reptile, not a mammal.

Dromaeosaurus

THE FACTS

MEANING:	Runner lizard
DATE:	Late Cretaceous
GROUP:	Theropoda
DIET:	Meat
SIZE:	6 feet (1.8 m) long
FOSSIL LOCATIONS:	USA, Canada 1922

Dryosaurus

PRONUNCIATION: DRY-o-SAW-rus

This plant eater may have grown up to be large, but most specimens are small. *Dryosaurus* was a lightly built dinosaur and its only defense was to run away. Therefore, it is possible that many animals died young. Its teeth were distinctive—they had long roots and leaf-shaped crowns. They were designed to cut up leaves and other soft vegetation. Its main problem was how to avoid getting stepped on by *Diplodocus*, *Camarasaurus*, and *Brachiosaurus*, who were all 30 times bigger.

THE FACTS

MEANING: Oak lizard

DATE: Late Jurassic

GROUP: Ornithopoda

DIET: Plants

SIZE: 10–13 feet (3–4 m) long

FOSSIL LOCATIONS: USA, Tanzania 1894

Dryosaurus

Edmontonia

PRONUNCIATION: ed-mon-TOH-nee-a

This dinosaur had bands of flexible armor along its back and looked like a living tank. Its shoulders had double spikes and were designed to be rammed into the leg of a tyrannosaur. Its body was covered with thick skin, bony bumps, and spikes. Despite its large size, its teeth were as small as those of a human baby. One scientist suggested that the reason why *Edmontonia* was completely encased in armor was to protect itself against its main food source—ants and termites.

Edmontonia had a boxlike head, with a set of interlocking bony plates over the upper surfaces to protect its brain, eyes, and nose.

Edmontonia

THE FACTS

MEANING: From Edmonton (Canada)

DATE: Late Cretaceous

GROUP: Ankylosauria

DIET: Plants

SIZE: 23 feet (7 m) long

FOSSIL LOCATIONS: USA, Canada 1928

Edmontosaurus

PRONUNCIATION: ed-MONT-oh-SAW-rus

Edmontosaurus was a non-crested duckbill dinosaur. Skulls have been found that are more than 3 feet (1 m) long, with more than 720 diamond-shaped teeth interlocked into a "dental battery." Its teeth were ever-sharpening and ever-replacing so, in a lifetime, a duckbill could go through more than 10,000 teeth. The upper and lower tooth batteries were angled to form a natural grinding surface. The beak was made from a large sheath of hornlike substance that overlapped the lower jaw to form a blade.

Edmontosaurus had rows of tiny teeth in the back of its mouth that acted like a cheese grater.

Edmontosaurus

Einiosaurus

PRONUNCIATION: eye-nee-o-SAW-rus

This large plant eater lived about 75 million years ago. It had a nose horn that looked like a giant, old-fashioned can opener. Its skull was held close to the ground and its horn may have been used somehow in feeding—it definitely served as a defensive weapon. The two spikes sticking out from its frill protected its backbone. Its name means "buffalo lizard" but *Einiosaurus* was much slower than a buffalo and it could not gallop.

THE FACTS
MEANING: Buffalo lizard
DATE: Late Cretaceous
GROUP: Ceratopsia
DIET: Plants
SIZE: 20 feet (6 m) long
FOSSIL LOCATIONS: USA 1995

Einiosaurus

THE FACTS

MEANING: Dawn shark

DATE: Early Cretaceous

GROUP: Theropoda

DIET: Meat

SIZE: 23 feet (7 m) long

FOSSIL LOCATIONS: Niger 2008

Eocarcharia

PRONUNCIATION: EE-oh-car-KAIR-ee-a

This theropod lived in Niger, Africa 110 million years ago. It had bladelike teeth that could rip its prey apart. Its prominent bony eyebrow and the roof of its skull were made of thick bone—thicker than in other theropods. This could mean that these dinosaurs butted heads during mating season. *Eocarcharia* was much smaller than its later relative *Carcharodontosaurus*.

Eocarcharia

THE FACTS

MEANING: Dawn runner

DATE: Late Triassic

GROUP: Ornithopoda

DIET: Plants

SIZE: 3 feet (1 m) long

FOSSIL LOCATIONS: South Africa 2007

Eocursor

PRONUNCIATION: EE-oh-Kur-sore

Eocursor was a small two-legged plant eater that lived during the late Triassic. It may not have been a true ornithopod but, instead, it may have been part of a group that were ornithopod's ancestors. Its teeth were like those of a living iguana's and were adapted to eating both plants and insects. Its shinbone was longer than its thighbone, which was a good indication that speed was its best defense.

Eocursor

Eoraptor

PRONUNCIATION: EE-oh-RAP-tor

This dog-size predator was perhaps the most primitive of all known dinosaurs. Some scientists think it was one of the first theropods. Because of its large, grasping hands, this active, fast-moving hunter may have been able to catch prey almost as large as itself. It ran mainly on its hind limbs but may have sometimes walked on all fours.

THE FACTS

MEANING:	Dawn thief
DATE:	Late Triassic
GROUP:	Theropoda
DIET:	Meat
SIZE:	3 feet (1 m) long
FOSSIL LOCATIONS:	Argentina 1993

◻ *Eoraptor*

Eotyrannus

PRONUNCIATION: EE-oh-ti-RAN-us

Eotyrannus had one feature in common with all the tyrannosaurs. If you take one of its main teeth and cut it, separating the top and bottom halves, the resulting cross section looks like the letter "D." No other group of theropods has this feature. Unlike the most famous member of this group, *Tyrannosaurus rex*, *Eotyrannus*'s fingers were long and useful for grabbing prey.

THE FACTS

MEANING:	Dawn tyrant
DATE:	Early Cretaceous
GROUP:	Theropoda
DIET:	Meat
SIZE:	20 feet (6m) long
FOSSIL LOCATIONS:	England 2001

◻ *Eotyrannus*

Equijubus

PRONUNCIATION: ee-kwi-JUH-bus

This Asian plant eater lived 110 million years ago. Its skull was halfway between an iguanodont dinosaur, such as *Iguanodon*, and a duckbill. It did not have a crest but it did have more than one row of teeth—most duckbills and horned dinosaurs had two or three rows but other dinosaurs usually had only one. The existence of *Equijubus* seems to confirm that duckbill dinosaurs first evolved in Asia.

Equijubus

THE FACTS

MEANING: Horse mane

DATE: Early Cretaceous

GROUP: Ornithopoda

DIET: Plants

SIZE: 26 feet (8 m) long

FOSSIL LOCATIONS: China 2003

Erketu

PRONUNCIATION: err-KEH-too

This sauropod is known for its long neck, which was twice as long as its body. Its heavy body counterbalanced the weight of its neck. *Erketu* had two sets of spines on top of its neck, instead of the usual single set. Muscles ran between its vertebrae to hold up its neck—this same system is used in suspension bridges today.

THE FACTS

MEANING: Mighty deity

DATE: Early Cretaceous

GROUP: Sauropodamorpha

DIET: Plants

SIZE: 98 feet (30 m) long

FOSSIL LOCATIONS: Mongolia 2006

Erketu

Euoplocephalus

PRONUNCIATION: yoo-oh-ploh-SEF-uh-lus

Euoplocephalus is the dinosaur most people picture when they think of an ankylosaur—a tanklike dinosaur. Several of its last tailbones were fused together and covered in bone to form a massive tail club. If an adult swung its tail it could have shattered a tyrannosaur's knee. If surrounded, *Euoplocephalus* simply dropped to the ground so that only its bite-proof armor was visible.

Euoplocephalus

THE FACTS

MEANING: Well armored head

DATE: Late Cretaceous

GROUP: Ankylosauria

DIET: Plants

SIZE: 26 feet (8 m) long

FOSSIL LOCATIONS: USA, Canada 1910

The most lethal weapon in *Euoplocephalus*'s armory was the double-headed club at the end of its long, stiffened tail.

Europasaurus

PRONUNCIATION: yoo-ROPE-ah-SAW-rus

This sauropod from the late Jurassic is believed to have been a dwarf species. Dwarfing occurred when animals were isolated on islands where their food supply was limited. The smaller the animal, the less food it needed to survive, and the less it grew. There were many large islands in Europe during this time where animals could become stranded.

Europasaurus

THE FACTS

MEANING: Lizard from Europe

DATE: Late Jurassic

GROUP: Sauropodamorpha

DIET: Plants

SIZE: 20 feet (6 m) long

FOSSIL LOCATIONS: Germany 2006

Euskelosaurus

THE FACTS

MEANING: Good leg lizard

DATE: Late Triassic

GROUP: Sauropodamorpha

DIET: Plants

SIZE: 29 feet (9 m) long

FOSSIL LOCATIONS: South Africa, Zimbabwe, Lesotho 1866

PRONUNCIATION: yoo-SKEL-uh-SAW-rus

Euskelosaurus was one of the largest and heaviest prosauropods. It was closely related to the first giant sauropod, *Plateosaurus*—both dinosaurs lived in the supercontinent of Pangea. The prosauropods were somewhere between meat-eating and plant-eating dinosaurs. *Euskelosaurus*'s teeth could process both meat and plants. Its thighbones were bowed outward from its body, perhaps because it needed a bigger gut area to process plants.

Euskelosaurus

Eustreptospondylus

PRONUNCIATION: yoo-STREP-toh-SPON-dee-lus

This meat eater had a hip height of 6 feet (2 m). It was a typical theropod with long arms, three clawed fingers on each hand, a stiffened tail, and relatively small, but serrated, teeth. At the time it was alive, western Europe had many small islands and lagoons in well-watered environments. This made an excellent hunting ground for *Eustreptospondylus*.

Eustreptospondylus

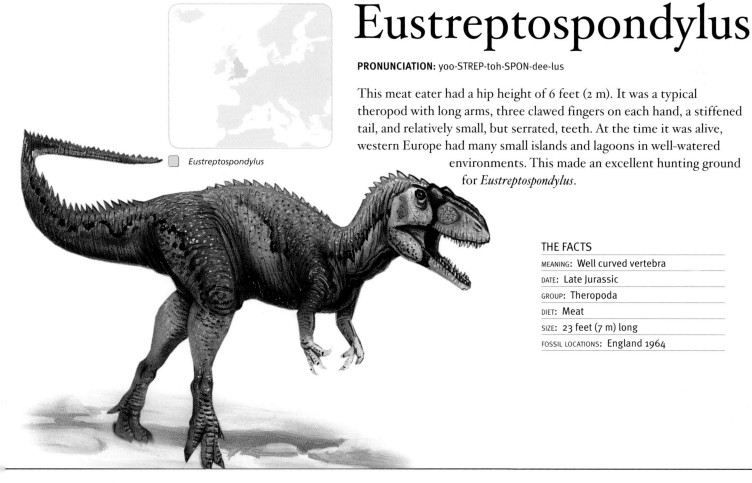

THE FACTS

MEANING: Well curved vertebra

DATE: Late Jurassic

GROUP: Theropoda

DIET: Meat

SIZE: 23 feet (7 m) long

FOSSIL LOCATIONS: England 1964

Fabrosaurus

PRONUNCIATION: FAB-roh-SAW-rus

This small plant-eating dinosaur was one of the first ornithischians. However, *Fabrosaurus* may become "extinct" for a second time! Its name was based on only a few teeth fossils— *Fabrosaurus* may be the same as *Lesothosaurus*, another plant eater. The description of *Lesothosaurus* is based on better specimens. Scientists call *Fabrosaurus* a *nomen dubium*, or, a "dubious name for scientific use."

THE FACTS

MEANING: Fabre's lizard

DATE: Early Jurassic

GROUP: Ornithopoda

DIET: Plants

SIZE: 3 feet (1 m) long

FOSSIL LOCATIONS: South Africa, Lesotho 1964

Fabrosaurus

Falcarius

PRONUNCIATION: fal-KAIR-ree-us

This is an early therizinosaur— a bizarre group of theropods that had both plant-eater and meat-eater bone structures. *Falcarius* had wide hips, leaf-shape teeth, and a long neck—like a plant eater. It also had 5-inch (12-cm) sickle claws, a two-legged posture, and feathers—like a meat eater. It was found in a 2-acre (8,000-sq m) bed of fossils in Utah, USA. Hundreds of specimens have been found but only a few have been studied.

Falcarius

THE FACTS

MEANING: Sickle

DATE: Early Cretaceous

GROUP: Theropoda

DIET: Meat

SIZE: 13 feet (4 m) long

FOSSIL LOCATIONS: USA 2005

Fukuiraptor

THE FACTS

MEANING: Fukui (province in Japan) thief

DATE: Early Cretaceous

GROUP: Theropoda

DIET: Meat

SIZE: 14 feet (4.2 m) long

FOSSIL LOCATIONS: Japan 2000

PRONUNCIATION: foo-KOO-ee-RAP-tor

Even though this was a Cretaceous dinosaur, it was a member of a group of dinosaurs mostly from the Jurassic. It weighed about 386 pounds (175 kg) and was a fast-moving meat eater. The information on this dinosaur is based on part of a skeleton and this may have been from a teenager—*Fukuiraptor* may have grown much bigger. It had relatively large hands, which were comparatively larger than *Allosaurus*'s hands in proportion to its body.

Fukuiraptor

Fukuisaurus

THE FACTS

MEANING: Fukui (province in Japan) lizard

DATE: Early Cretaceous

GROUP: Ornithopoda

DIET: Plants

SIZE: 16 feet (5 m) long

FOSSIL LOCATIONS: Japan 2003

PRONUNCIATION: foo-KOO-ee-SAW-rus

The information on this rare dinosaur is based on parts of skulls of young dinosaurs. It had a short face and only 20 rows of teeth per jaw, which meant it was not fully grown. One unique feature of this plant eater was that it did not have a "mobile" skull. That is, its upper and lower jaws did not move independently of each other as it ground up plants. Having an upper jaw that did not move was unusual for this kind of dinosaur.

Fukuisaurus

Futalongkosaurus

PRONUNCIATION: FOO-ta-long-koh-SAW-rus

Futalongkosaurus was a titanosaur, the last great group of sauropods to appear. It had a wide, thick body that counterbalanced its long neck, which it held high to feed on tall trees. Adults probably pulled down branches for young dinosaurs who were too short to reach. When the young grew to about one year old, they fed on bushes.

THE FACTS

MEANING: Giant chief lizard

DATE: Late Cretaceous

GROUP: Sauropodamorpha

DIET: Plants

SIZE: 110 feet (33 m) long

FOSSIL LOCATIONS: Argentina 2007

Futalongkosaurus

TRUE GIANTS

There are several dinosaurs lining up to claim the title of the "biggest." The leader, so far, is *Amphicoelias* at 196 feet (60 m), followed by *Bruhathkayosaurus* at 144 feet (44 m). Then comes *Argentinosaurus* at 115 feet (35 m). However, none of these sauropods is based on complete fossils, only partial skeletons.

Gallimimus

THE FACTS

MEANING: Fowl (bird) mimic

DATE: Late Cretaceous

GROUP: Theropoda

DIET: Plants and some meat

SIZE: 17 feet (5 m) long

FOSSIL LOCATIONS: Mongolia 1972

☐ Gallimimus

PRONUNCIATION: GAL-ee-MY-mus

This theropod stood about twice as high as an adult human. It was one of the fastest dinosaurs and could outrun a tyrannosaur. Its eyes were relatively large, possibly for hunting mammals at night. They also faced to the side, so they had a wide range of vision but not good depth perception. *Gallimimus* had a beak and no teeth, which means it probably ate both plants and animals. Its arms were long and could easily reach the ground to grab plants, mammals, lizards, and other small prey. At more than 6 feet (2 m) tall and 17 feet (5 m) long, *Gallimimus* was the biggest ornithomimid.

Gallimimus had a sharp, narrow beak. This was perfect for catching food such as insects, small animals, or eggs that it could swallow in one gulp.

FAST MOVER

Gallimimus is running away from *Albertosaurus* and there is no way the lumbering *Albertosaurus* can catch it. *Gallimimus* could reach speeds of 30 miles per hour (48 kph). It was also able to change direction quickly, dodging and weaving out of reach.

Gargoyleosaurus

PRONUNCIATION: gar-GOYL-o-SAW-rus

This was one of the earliest known ankylosaurs and one of only two, so far, from the Jurassic. It had a shield over its pelvis and large, hollow, pointed skin armor on its back. This armor looked similar to that of a modern lizard, such as a moloch or a thorny devil. A set of sideway-facing spikes ran along each side of its body. Unusually, the front part of its mouth had seven teeth—most ankylosaurs had no teeth in the front of their beaks.

THE FACTS

MEANING: Gargoyle lizard

DATE: Late Jurassic

GROUP: Ankylosauria

DIET: Plants

SIZE: 10 feet (3 m) long

FOSSIL LOCATIONS: USA 1998

Gargoyleosaurus

GIANT HUNTER

Giganotosaurus lived alongside several giant sauropods. It was the only theropod in the region large enough to attack sauropods from above. Several *Giganotosaurus* skeletons have been found close together, which suggests they may have moved and hunted in groups.

Giganotosaurus

THE FACTS

MEANING: For (Robert) Gaston

DATE: Early Cretaceous

GROUP: Ankylosauria

DIET: Plants

SIZE: 15 feet (4.5 m) long

FOSSIL LOCATIONS: USA 1998

Gastonia

PRONUNCIATION: gas-TOH-nee-a

Gastonia had a shield over its pelvis and large, pointed spikes along its back. A set of small, sideway-facing spikes ran all the way down its tail. This armor was used to fight off predators, such as *Utahraptor*, which has been found in the same area. *Gastonia* was one of the most heavily decorated ankylosaurs but it did not have a tail club.

Gastonia

Giganotosaurus

PRONUNCIATION: jig-a-NOT-o-SAW-rus

Giganotosaurus was one of the largest theropods ever to walk Earth. Its skull alone was 6 feet (2 m) long. There is strong competition for the title of "largest predatory dinosaur of all time" between this dinosaur, *Carcharodontosaurus*, and *Tyrannosaurus*. The winner is still unknown. Scientists have found fossils of all three, which are waiting to be studied. This name is often confused with *Gigantosaurus*, which is a sauropod.

THE FACTS

MEANING: Giant southern lizard

DATE: Late Cretaceous

GROUP: Theropoda

DIET: Meat

SIZE: 43 feet (13 m) long

FOSSIL LOCATIONS: Argentina 1995

Gigantoraptor

PRONUNCIATION: jahy-GAN-toe-RAP-tor

This giant birdlike dinosaur was 15 feet (5 m) tall and weighed 1.6 tons (1.5 t). Studies of its bone tell scientists that it was not fully grown. It had a toothless beak and claws. Although no feathers were found with the bones, they were common in this kind of dinosaur. It was nearly the same size as *Tyrannosaurus* but was more agile and faster because it was lighter. This dinosaur was discovered by Chinese paleontologist Xu Xing while filming a television special on another dinosaur.

THE FACTS

MEANING: Giant thief

DATE: Late Cretaceous

GROUP: Theropoda

DIET: Meat

SIZE: 25 feet (8 m) long

FOSSIL LOCATIONS: Mongolia, China 2007

Gigantoraptor

Gojirasaurus

PRONUNCIATION: go-JHEE-ra-SAW-rus

Gojirasaurus is more famous for its name than for its bones. "Gojira" is the original name for the "King of the Dinosaurs," in America the name was changed to "Godzilla." At the time it was alive, it may have been the largest predator in North America. It probably weighed about 440 pounds (200 kg). *Gojirasaurus* was a member of the first major group of theropods to appear and they were all relatively small.

THE FACTS

MEANING: Gojira (Godzilla) lizard

DATE: Late Triassic

GROUP: Theropoda

DIET: Meat

SIZE: 18 feet (5.5 m) long

FOSSIL LOCATIONS: New Mexico, USA 1997

Gojirasaurus

Guanlong

Guanlong

THE FACTS

MEANING: Crown dragon

DATE: Late Jurassic

GROUP: Theropoda

DIET: Meat

SIZE: 10 feet (3 m) long

FOSSIL LOCATIONS: China 2006

PRONUNCIATION: GWAN-long

Guanlong lived about 160 million years ago in the late Jurassic. It was one of the earliest tyrannosaurs, which were mostly from the late Cretaceous. *Guanlong* had three long fingers on each hand, unlike other tyrannosaurs that had only two. Its unique feature was the crest on top of its head. It was as large as its snout area and about 2.5 inches (6 cm) high but it was delicate and too thin to be used in combat. It was probably only used for display—either to attract a mate or to be identified as a *Guanlong*.

FAMILY TIES

Guanlong was closely related to *Dilong* and may have had feathers as this dinosaur did. It was about 4 feet (1.2 m) tall at the hips—about a third of the size of its other relative, *Tyrannosaurus rex*.

Herrerasaurus

PRONUNCIATION: huh-RARE-uh-SAW-rus

According to some scientists this Triassic dinosaur from Argentina was one of the earliest theropods. According to others, it was not a dinosaur at all. The problem lies in its bones: only two of its vertebrae were attached to its hip bone—but dinosaurs had three vertebrae attached to their hip bones. So *Herrerasaurus* could not be a true theropod.

THE FACTS
MEANING:	Herrera's lizard
DATE:	Late Triassic
GROUP:	Theropoda
DIET:	Meat
SIZE:	6 feet (2 m) long
FOSSIL LOCATIONS:	Argentina 1963

Herrerasaurus

Heterodontosaurus

PRONUNCIATION: HET-uh-roh-DONT-o-SAW-rus

Normally, the teeth in a dinosaur's mouth all looked the same, but this dinosaur had three kinds of teeth. Its front teeth were designed to clip plants and, right behind them, where humans have canine teeth, it had a set of fangs. It also had teeth in its cheek area that were designed to chomp plants. As no other dinosaurs had fangs, scientists are still not sure how they were used. *Heterodontosaurus* probably displayed them to look threatening.

Heterodontosaurus had two pairs of large fangs, similar to the canines of a carnivore. They may have used them to dig up roots or to ward off rivals.

THE FACTS
MEANING:	Different tooth lizard
DATE:	Early Jurassic
GROUP:	Ceratopsia
DIET:	Plants
SIZE:	4 feet (1.2 m) long
FOSSIL LOCATIONS:	South Africa 1962

Heterodontosaurus

Huaxiagnathus

PRONUNCIATION: hwah-XIA-na-thus

This small Cretaceous theropod lived in China. It belonged to the same group as *Compsognathus*, a small Jurassic theropod. The most unusual feature about *Huaxiagnathus* was its long hand. The size of its hand and its overall build, made this dinosaur perfectly suited to grabbing small prey running along the ground.

THE FACTS
MEANING: Jaw from Hua Xia (China)
DATE: Early Cretaceous
GROUP: Theropoda
DIET: Meat
SIZE: 4 feet (1.2 m) long
FOSSIL LOCATIONS: China 2004

Huaxiagnathus

THE FACTS
MEANING: High-crested tooth
DATE: Early Cretaceous
GROUP: Ornithopoda
DIET: Plants
SIZE: 7 feet (2.1 m) long
FOSSIL LOCATIONS: England, Spain 1869

Hypsilophodon

PRONUNCIATION: hip-seh-LOF-o-don

Although this small plant eater lived in the early Cretaceous, it had features of dinosaurs from millions of years earlier. By the beginning of the Cretaceous, most plant eating dinosaurs had only three or four fingers but *Hypsilophodon* had five. Also, by this time, most plant eaters had beaks, which had replaced teeth, but *Hypsilophodon* had teeth. This made *Hypsilophodon* a "living fossil" in its own time.

Hypsilophodon

Iguanodon

PRONUNCIATION: ig-WAHN-o-don

This is one of the most well-known dinosaurs, and the second one to be scientifically named. Its most famous feature is its thumb spike, which probably took out the eye of more than one theropod. *Iguanodon* was one of the first dinosaurs to be reconstructed, in 1852, in London. In 1878, coal miners in Belgium, found a layer of rock full of fossils, or a bone bed, that contained more than 30 *Iguanodon* skeletons. In 1989 an asteroid was named in honor of this dinosaur.

THE FACTS

MEANING:	Iguana tooth
DATE:	Early Cretaceous
GROUP:	Ornithopoda
DIET:	Plants
SIZE:	33 feet (10 m) long
FOSSIL LOCATIONS:	England, Belgium, Germany, France, Spain 1825

Iguanodon

IMPORTANT FINDS

When Mary Ann Mantell, wife of the famous fossil hunter, Gideon Mantell, first found *Iguanodon* fossil teeth, her husband thought they belonged to an extinct reptile. Scientists told him they were rhinoceros teeth.

In 1822, Mary Ann Mantell found some *Iguanodon* teeth in a quarry.

In 1834, a large number of *Iguanodon* bones were discovered in a slab of rock.

Scientists had a much better idea of what *Iguanodon* looked like after more than 30 skeletons were discovered in 1878.

Iguanodon used its large spike as a dagger. Its three middle fingers had hoodlike claws, to take its weight when walking. Its fifth finger could bend and grasp plants and other objects.

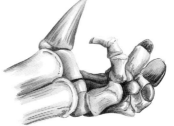

WELL TRAVELED

Iguanodon lived in herds, probably for protection. It was active and was possibly the most widespread of the dinosaurs. Specimens have been found in Africa, North America, Europe, Asia, and even the Arctic.

IGUANODON ANATOMY

Scientists first thought *Iguanodon* stood on its hind legs with its tail stretched out along the ground. New studies reveal that it had strong front legs and hooves, so it probably spent some time on all fours but ran on its hind legs.

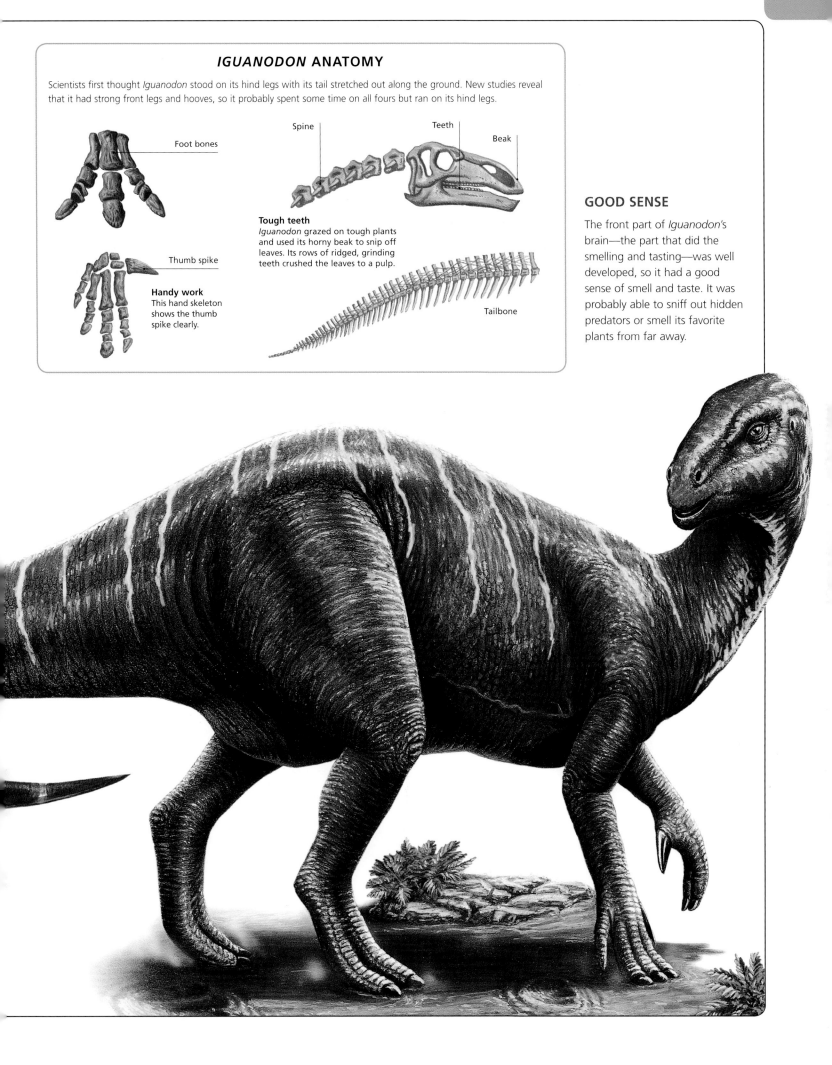

Foot bones

Spine

Teeth

Beak

Tough teeth
Iguanodon grazed on tough plants and used its horny beak to snip off leaves. Its rows of ridged, grinding teeth crushed the leaves to a pulp.

Thumb spike

Handy work
This hand skeleton shows the thumb spike clearly.

Tailbone

GOOD SENSE

The front part of *Iguanodon*'s brain—the part that did the smelling and tasting—was well developed, so it had a good sense of smell and taste. It was probably able to sniff out hidden predators or smell its favorite plants from far away.

Incisivosaurus

PRONUNCIATION: in-sai-see-vo-SAW-rus

This tiny birdlike theropod belonged to the same group as *Oviraptor*, but it was an earlier dinosaur. It had ratlike front teeth, instead of a toothless beak like its relatives—perhaps it was on the way to becoming a plant eater. *Incisivosaurus* had feathers and was about the size of a large bird. Its skull was only 4 inches (10 cm) long.

THE FACTS

MEANING: Incisor lizard

DATE: Early Cretaceous

GROUP: Theropoda

DIET: Meat

SIZE: 3 feet (1 m) long

FOSSIL LOCATIONS: China 2002

Incisivorsaurus

ODD ONE OUT

Most *Oviraptors* had no teeth but *Incisivosaurus* had enlarged "canines" up front plus peglike teeth in its cheek area. Many scientists think this dinosaur is the same dinosaur as *Protarchaeopteryx*.

THE FACTS

MEANING: Lizard from Jingshan (China)

DATE: Late Triassic

GROUP: Sauropodamorpha

DIET: Plants

SIZE: 25 feet (7.5 m) long

FOSSIL LOCATIONS: China 1995

Jingshanosaurus

PRONUNCIATION: JING-SHAHN-o-SAW-rus

Jingshanosaurus was one of the last prosauropods, which were the earliest dinosaurs. They were replaced in the Jurassic by sauropods. Its legs were thick and heavy and it had a long neck. Its skull was full of teeth that it used to eat thick, woody plant material. Scientists have found a nearly complete skeleton, a cast of which toured the USA in the 1990s.

Jingshanosaurus

THE FACTS

MEANING: Jurassic hunter

DATE: Late Jurassic

GROUP: Theropoda

DIET: Meat

SIZE: 2.3 feet (70 cm) long

FOSSIL LOCATIONS: Germany 2006

Juravenator

PRONUNCIATION: JOO-rah-ven-AY-tor

This tiny theropod was a coelurosaur—the ancestors of birds—from the Jurassic. The skeleton was from a young dinosaur. No feathers were found with the bones, even though there was a preserved patch of skin. So *Juravenator* probably belonged to a less advanced group of featherless theropods.

Juravenator

Kentrosaurus

PRONUNCIATION: KEN-tro-SAW-rus

This Jurassic dinosaur was closely related to the American *Stegosaurus*, but it lived in Tanzania. It had pairs of small plates along its neck and back, and pairs of small spikes along its hips and tail. It was less advanced than *Stegosaurus*. The original *Kentrosaurus* specimens were kept in a German museum. They were mostly destroyed by bombing during World War II.

THE FACTS

MEANING: Pointed lizard
DATE: Late Jurassic
GROUP: Stegosauria
DIET: Plants
SIZE: 16 feet (4.9 m) long
FOSSIL LOCATIONS: Tanzania 1915

☐ *Kentrosaurus*

Kerberosaurus

PRONUNCIATION: ker-BAIR-oh-SAW-rus

This solid-crested duckbill dinosaur lived near the end of the Mesozoic and was closely related to *Prosaurolophus*. North American duckbill dinosaurs from the same age were more advanced in their design. *Kerberosaurus* was from the Amur River in Russia. Travel between Asia and North America was easy at the end of the Mesozoic because these areas were still connected by land. Dinosaurs migrated across continents and evolved at different rates.

THE FACTS

MEANING: Kerberos lizard
DATE: Late Cretaceous
GROUP: Ornithopoda
DIET: Plants
SIZE: 30 feet (9 m) long
FOSSIL LOCATIONS: Russia 2004

☐ *Kerberosaurus*

Kryptops

THE FACTS

MEANING: Covered face

DATE: Early Cretaceous

GROUP: Theropoda

DIET: Meat

SIZE: 20 feet (6 m) long

FOSSIL LOCATIONS: Niger 2000

PRONUNCIATION: KRIP-tops

This abelisaur was one of the earliest and most primitive of its kind. It lived about 110 million years ago in Niger, Africa. It was only half as big as the later abelisaurs. Its face was covered with a bony coating. One of the fossils has an intact upper jawbone and the waiting replacement teeth can be seen inside the bone. This dinosaur lived at the same time as *Spinosaurus*, *Nigersaurus*, *Ouranosaurus*, and *Lurdusaurus*.

☐ *Kryptops*

Lambeosaurus

THE FACTS

MEANING: (Lawrence) Lambe's lizard

DATE: Late Cretaceous

GROUP: Ornithopoda

DIET: Plants

SIZE: 49 feet (15 m) long

FOSSIL LOCATIONS: Canada, USA 1923

PRONUNCIATION: LAM-bee-o-SAW-rus

This is one of the most famous hollow-crested duckbill dinosaurs. Unlike the non-crested duckbills, which had wide beaks, *Lambeosaurus* had a narrow beak—it had to be fussy about what it ate. It is named after Lawrence Lambe, a famous paleontologist who worked in Canada in the late 19th and early 20th centuries. Lambe discovered several new dinosaur species, including this one.

☐ *Lambeosaurus*

Leaellynasaura

PRONUNCIATION: lee-ELL-in-a-SAW-ruh

This little ornithopod was only 3 feet (1 m) long and would have found it difficult to keep warm. This is puzzling because it lived inside the Antarctic Circle (Australia was within the Antarctic Circle during the early Cretaceous). It spent months in darkness and had large eyes, which probably helped it see in the dark. *Leaellynasaura* was named by Australian paleontologists Pat Vickers Rich and Tom Rich after their daughter.

THE FACTS

MEANING: Leaellyn's lizard

DATE: Early Cretaceous

GROUP: Ornithopoda

DIET: Plants

SIZE: 3 feet (1 m) long

FOSSIL LOCATIONS: Australia 1989

Leaellynasaura

Liaoningosaurus

PRONUNCIATION: LYOW-ning-o-SAW-rus

The tiny fossil of this nodosaur, one of the two main groups of ankylosaurs, may have been a baby. Unlike any other ankylosaur, *Liaoningosaurus* had armor on its belly, not just on its back and sides. *Liaoningosaurus* was named after the province of Liaoning, in China, where the Yixian Formation is being excavated. The feathered dinosaurs of China were found in this same formation, which is known for its exceptional preservation of fossils.

THE FACTS

MEANING: Lizard from Liaoning (China)

DATE: Early Cretaceous

GROUP: Ankylosauria

DIET: Plants

SIZE: 1 foot (34 cm) long

FOSSIL LOCATIONS: China 2001

Liaoningosaurus

THE FACTS

MEANING: Good mother lizard

DATE: Late Cretaceous

GROUP: Ornithopoda

DIET: Plants

SIZE: 32 feet (10 m) long

FOSSIL LOCATIONS: USA 1979

Maiasaura took good care of their young and are known as nurturers. Females nested in large groups.

Maiasaura

PRONUNCIATION: MAY-a-SAW-ruh

This duckbill dinosaur is the official state fossil of Montana. It was also the first dinosaur nest with babies to be found in the USA. By studying the babies and adults, scientists found that it took only one year for *Maiasaura* to grow to 3 feet (1 m) long—adults were 32 feet (10 m) long. Such a rapid growth rate tells us that this dinosaur used much more energy than today's reptiles use.

☐ *Maiasaura*

THE FACTS

MEANING: Lizard from Mahajanga (Madagascar)

DATE: Late Cretaceous

GROUP: Theropoda

DIET: Meat

SIZE: 26 feet (8 m) long

FOSSIL LOCATIONS: Madagascar 1955

Majungasaurus

PRONUNCIATION: mah-JOONG-ah-SAW-rus

Majungasaurus is known from many skeletons and a complete, intact skull. Its neck and snout were thick and strong. In one specimen the end of its tail had been bitten off. *Majungasaurus* belonged to a relatively primitive group of theropods, and the sauropod *Rapetosaurus* was probably its favorite prey. There is evidence that it may have also been a cannibal. *Majungasaurus* was found in Madagascar, which was already an island by the end of the Cretaceous.

☐ *Majungasaurus*

Mamenchisaurus

PRONUNCIATION: mah-MEN-kee-SAW-rus

This Chinese dinosaur lived in the Jurassic. Its neck was up to 40 feet (12 m) long—it had a series of hollow chambers on each side of each neck bone that made its neck lighter. These chambers are also found in theropods and are still found in birds. *Mamenchisaurus*'s long neck was counter-balanced by its body and tail. It could eat the soft foliage from treetops that were too high for other sauropods.

Mamenchisaurus

THE FACTS

MEANING:	Lizard from Mamenchi (China)
DATE:	Late Jurassic
GROUP:	Sauropodamorpha
DIET:	Plants
SIZE:	82 feet (25 m) long
FOSSIL LOCATIONS:	China 1954

Masiakasaurus

PRONUNCIATION: mah-SHEE-ah-kah-SAW-rus

This theropod from the late Cretaceous is an abelisaur. The abelisaurs were common on all the southern continents when these were one landmass, Gondwana. *Masiakasaurus* is noted for its unique jaw and tooth structure. The tip of both jaws curved outward, making it look as if its teeth pointed forward. These small teeth were adapted for grabbing, not ripping or tearing as in other large theropods.

THE FACTS

MEANING:	Vicious lizard
DATE:	Late Cretaceous
GROUP:	Theropod
DIET:	Meat
SIZE:	6 feet (1.8 m) long
FOSSIL LOCATIONS:	Madagascar 2001

Masiakasaurus

Massospondylus

PRONUNCIATION: mass-o-SPON-di-lus

Massospondylus

This prosauropod was named by Sir Richard Owen, the famous paleontologist who made up the word "Dinosauria" in 1842. Its hind legs were much longer than its front legs, but its hands had a large claw that would have made walking on them impossible. *Massospondylus* probably walked on two legs but rested on all four. Its teeth and jaws were adapted to eat mostly plants but it may have eaten small animals and scavenged flesh that could be swallowed whole.

THE FACTS

MEANING: Elongated vertebra

DATE: Early Jurassic

GROUP: Sauropodamorpha

DIET: Plants

SIZE: 16 feet (5 m) long

FOSSIL LOCATIONS: Southern Africa, Lesotho, Zimbabwe 1854

Massospondylus had enlarged sickle-like thumb claws on each hand. These could have been used to ward off predators as it reared on its hind legs.

Megalosaurus

PRONUNCIATION: MEG-a-lo-SAW-rus

Megalosaurus had powerful hinged jaws and curved, serrated teeth—all signs of a fierce predator.

Megalosaurus

Megalosaurus was the first dinosaur to be scientifically named, in 1824. Unfortunately, it was not based on a complete skeleton and there is little known about it. For a long time any partial theropod bones from the Cretaceous that were found in Europe were said to be from *Megalosaurus*. What we do know is that it was a medium-size predator.

THE FACTS

MEANING: Great lizard

DATE: Late Jurassic

GROUP: Theropoda

DIET: Meat

SIZE: 30 feet (9 m) long

FOSSIL LOCATIONS: England 1822

Mei

PRONUNCIATION: MAY

If only all discoveries were as spectacular as this dinosaur!
This fossil was found in a sleeping position with its head tucked
under its forearm—a pose typical of resting birds today. It probably
suffocated quickly from poisonous volcanic gases. The specimen
is preserved almost completely intact, only slightly crushed.
It must have been a baby because its skull bones were not yet fused.

Mei

THE FACTS

MEANING: Soundly sleeping (dragon)

DATE: Early Cretaceous

GROUP: Theropoda

DIET: Meat

SIZE: 1½–3 feet (0.5–1 m) long

FOSSIL LOCATIONS: China 2004

SLEEPING BEAUTY

Scientists had never before found a sleeping
dinosaur fossil. This perfectly preserved
130-million-year-old skeleton was found curled
up in the same way today's birds do.

Microraptor

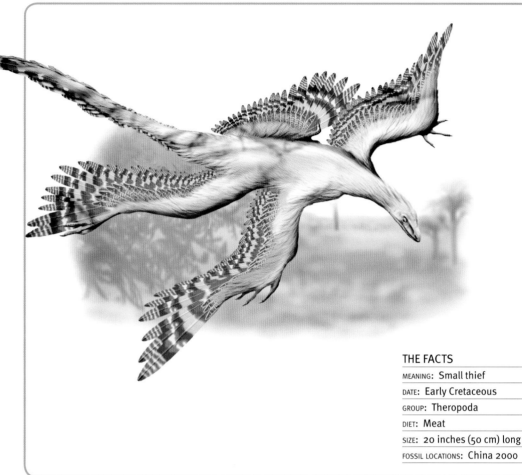

PRONUNCIATION: MY-kro-RAP-tor

The most unusual thing about this small dinosaur was its feathered hind limbs. The long and tapered feathers came from its thighbones and shinbones and made *Microraptor* look as if it had four wings. Further studies showed that the "hind wings" did not provide any lifting power and would not have been used for true flight. It is possible they were used for gliding.

THE FACTS

MEANING: Small thief

DATE: Early Cretaceous

GROUP: Theropoda

DIET: Meat

SIZE: 20 inches (50 cm) long

FOSSIL LOCATIONS: China 2000

☐ *Microraptor*

Minmi

☐ *Minmi*

PRONUNCIATION: MIN-mee

This ankylosaur from Queensland, Australia, had relatively small armor. Most ankylosaurs had armor lined up in bands that ran from side to side. *Minmi* had armor strips that ran from front to back. The armor on its belly was made of small, hexagonal, pebble-like bony plates, called scutes. Ankylosaurs migrated to Australia during the Jurassic, before the southern continent, Gondwana, started to split apart.

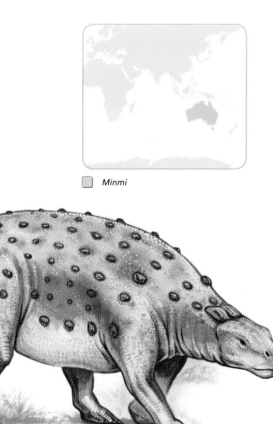

THE FACTS

MEANING: Lizard from Minmi Crossing (Australia)

DATE: Early Cretaceous

GROUP: Ankylosauria

DIET: Plants

SIZE: 8 feet (2.5 m) long

FOSSIL LOCATIONS: Australia 1980

Mononykus

PRONUNCIATION: mon-o-NEE-kus

The unique feature of this bird-size theropod was the single claw on the end of each arm. Its arms were held out to the side and were so short that the claws would not have reached its mouth. One theory is that its arms were used to dig into termite mounds. Its small teeth, which had no cutting edges, support this idea.

THE FACTS

MEANING:	Single (one) claw
DATE:	Late Cretaceous
GROUP:	Theropoda
DIET:	Meat
SIZE:	3 feet (1 m) long
FOSSIL LOCATIONS:	Mongolia 1993

Mononykus

Mononykus had graceful hind limbs but its arms were extremely short and its hands were reduced to a single digit—a clawed thumb.

Muttaburrasaurus

PRONUNCIATION: MUT-uh-BUH-ruh-SAW-rus

This large and unusual ornithopod from Australia had an expanded nose area, similar to a hadrosaur's, and a thumb claw that was like an iguanodont's. It also had shearing teeth, unlike other ornithopods. This mixture of unusual features has made it difficult to place *Muttaburrasaurus* in any of the known ornithopod families.

THE FACTS

MEANING:	Lizard from Muttaburra (Australia)
DATE:	Early Cretaceous
GROUP:	Ornithopoda
DIET:	Plants
SIZE:	33 feet (10 m) long
FOSSIL LOCATIONS:	Australia 1981

Muttaburrasaurus

Nigersaurus

PRONUNCIATION: nee-JUH-SAW-rus

Nigersaurus

Nigersaurus was a sauropod with a mouth shaped like the straight-edge head of a vacuum cleaner. It had more than 80 small teeth lined in a row. Behind each tooth was a set of more teeth stacked in a column, ready to pop into place when needed. As each tooth wore out, it was shed and the next tooth in line took its place. Its teeth were so small it must have eaten only soft-fiber plants.

THE FACTS

MEANING:	Lizard from Niger
DATE:	Early Cretaceous
GROUP:	Sauropodamorpha
DIET:	Plants
SIZE:	50 feet (15 m) long
FOSSIL LOCATIONS:	Niger 1999

Nomingia

PRONUNCIATION: no-MING-ee-a

Nomingia

This theropod was the first dinosaur found with a pygostyle—a group of fused vertebrae that formed the base for a fan of tail feathers. This fan could have been made of ornamental feathers or feathers that controlled flight. Tail fans were particularly important while flying at low speeds and during landing. However, *Nomingia*'s tail fan was too big to be used for flying, so its tail feathers were probably ornamental.

THE FACTS

MEANING:	From Nomingiin (Gobi Desert)
DATE:	Late Cretaceous
GROUP:	Theropoda
DIET:	Meat
SIZE:	5.5 feet (1.7 m) long
FOSSIL LOCATIONS:	Mongolia 2000

Ornitholestes

PRONUNCIATION: ORN-ith-oh-LESS-tees

Ornitholestes was a Jurassic theropod from the famous Morrison Formation in the USA. Most of what we know about this dinosaur is based on one skull and a skeleton collected more than 100 years ago. Since that time, no more complete fossils have been found. Its hands could be held so that the palms faced each other. This made it easier to grab and hold small prey. We do not know if this dinosaur had feathers.

☐ *Ornitholestes*

This skull shows a possible horn. Some reconstructions of *Ornitholestes* have a thin horn right above its nose.

THE FACTS

MEANING:	Bird robber
DATE:	Late Jurassic
GROUP:	Theropoda
DIET:	Meat
SIZE:	6 feet (2 m) long
FOSSIL LOCATIONS:	USA 1903

Oryctodromeus

PRONUNCIATION: or-IK-to-DRO-mee-us

This small dinosaur weighed about 66 pounds (30 kg). It was the first known ornithopod to be found inside its burrow. Two juveniles were found with one adult, still inside the burrow, indicating that this family died together. It also means that adult *Oryctodromeus* cared for their young. Their arms and head show some adaptations to digging, but not to the same extent that dedicated burrowers do today.

☐ *Oryctodromeus*

THE FACTS

MEANING:	Digging runner
DATE:	Late Cretaceous
GROUP:	Ornithopoda
DIET:	Plants
SIZE:	6 feet (2 m) long
FOSSIL LOCATIONS:	USA 2007

Ouranosaurus

PRONUNCIATION: OO-RAN-oh-SAW-rus

This ornithopod had a large "sail" on its back, made up of spines extending upward from the backbone. This sail was too fragile to protect the dinosaur so it was probably used for display. However, it could also have helped control the dinosaur's body temperature. If it stood in the shade—especially if its skin was wet—heat would have radiated out of its body. This would have helped cool down this 2-ton (1.8 t) plant eater.

Ouranosaurus

As *Ouranosaurus* closed its mouth, the bones in its upper jaw moved apart and broke up food with bands of cheek teeth.

THE FACTS

MEANING: Valiant lizard

DATE: Early Cretaceous

GROUP: Ornithopoda

DIET: Plants

SIZE: 23 feet (7 m) long

FOSSIL LOCATIONS: Niger 1976

Ouranosaurus is known from an almost complete skeleton. This skeleton shows the bones that supported its sail.

BUMPY ISSUE

Some scientists believe that *Ouranosaurus* did not need its hump to regulate its temperature. Its spines resemble those that form the withers in mammals such as bison. Was it a dinosaurian version of a camel or buffalo?

Oviraptor

PRONUNCIATION: oh-vee-RAP-tor

When it was first named, in 1924, this theropod was thought to have died while robbing a nest of *Protoceratops* eggs. Now scientists know that it was protecting its own eggs. Specimens have been found with adults sitting on top of eggs in a nest, their feathered arms folded over to protect the eggs. *Oviraptors* had a wide variety of crest shapes that changed depending on how old they were. It had two toothlike structures in the roof of its mouth and its beak had no real teeth behind it.

Dinosaur crests were varied and changed constantly during the animal's lifetime.

Oviraptor was initially branded an "egg thief" but scientists now believe it was looking after its own eggs, not stealing them.

THE FACTS

MEANING:	Egg thief
DATE:	Late Cretaceous
GROUP:	Theropoda
DIET:	Meat and plants
SIZE:	10 feet (3 m) long
FOSSIL LOCATIONS:	China, Mongolia 1924

☐ *Oviraptor*

DINNER TIME

A mother *Oviraptor* returns to her nest of hungry babies. She has a freshly killed baby *Velociraptor* for their dinner. Scientists have found *Oviraptor* skeletons sitting on nests with their forelimbs wrapped around the eggs. These were probably parents incubating and protecting their own eggs.

THE FACTS

MEANING: Thick-headed lizard

DATE: Late Cretaceous

GROUP: Pachycephalosauria

DIET: Plants

SIZE: 26 feet (8 m) long

FOSSIL LOCATIONS: USA 1943

Pachycephalosaurus

PRONUNCIATION: PAK-ee-kef-AH-loh-SAW-rus

Pachycephalosaurus is the defining dinosaur for the group of domeheads known as pachycephalosaurs, "thick-headed lizards." Some domes were up to 7 inches (18 cm) thick. It was once thought that the dome was used to ram other males but, if so, both dinosaurs would have been in danger of breaking their necks. Today most scientists think the dome was used to ram the legs or necks of theropods. The dome would have been at the level of a tyrannosaur's knee.

Pachycephalosaurus

Parasaurolophus

PRONUNCIATION: PAR-uh-SAW-roh-LOH-fus

This hadrosaur was the trombone of the Cretaceous. The large hollow crest above its head was formed from its upper-lip bone. Air entered its nose, traveled along the top of the hollow tube, looped around the bottom of the tube, then passed into its throat. Reconstructions of the tube show that *Parasaurolophus* made low-frequency sounds that carried for miles, as elephants do today. These sounds conveyed information between herds, such as "I found water" or "I just saw a tyrannosaur."

Parasaurolophus

THE FACTS

MEANING: Near (like a) crested lizard

DATE: Late Cretaceous

GROUP: Ornithopoda

DIET: Plants

SIZE: 35 feet (11 m) long

FOSSIL LOCATIONS: Canada, USA 1922

Pelecanimimus

PRONUNCIATION: pel-e-KAN-i-MY-mus

This unusual ornithomimosaur—a group of fast ostrich-like dinosaurs—had more than 220 teeth. Most dinosaurs in this group had no teeth. The large number of small teeth acted like a fine cutting tool and, possibly, were used for filtering food from the water. It had a strong tongue. Its hand was long, with three fingers that acted together as a hook. Some skin impressions have been found but no true feathers.

THE FACTS

MEANING: **Pelican mimic**

DATE: **Early Cretaceous**

GROUP: **Theropoda**

DIET: **Meat**

SIZE: **6–8 feet (2–2.5 m) long**

FOSSIL LOCATIONS: **Spain 1994**

□ *Pelecanimimus*

PELICAN POUCH

One of the most prominent features of *Pelecanimimus* was the unusual skin folds underneath its throat. These may have formed a pouch, similar to that of a pelican's.

Plateosaurus

THE FACTS

MEANING: Flat lizard

DATE: Late Triassic

GROUP: Sauropodamorpha

DIET: Plants and some animals

SIZE: 26 feet (8 m) long

FOSSIL LOCATIONS: Germany, France, Switzerland, Greenland 1837

PRONUNCIATION: PLAY-tee-oh-SAW-rus

Plateosaurus is the most famous of the prosauropods, which was the first giant sauropod. Its skull was long and its teeth were designed for eating plants, but they were thick enough for the occasional meal of small animals. Several skulls had the same bones that are found in living raptors, which help the animal to focus their eyes. It had large claws and its hind limbs were large and strong enough to support its heavy body when it reared up on two legs.

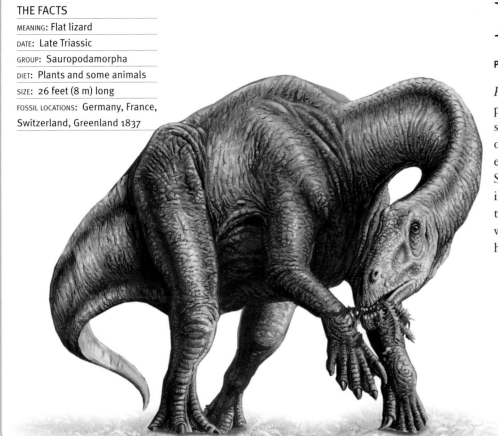

Plateosaurus

Prosaurolophus

THE FACTS

MEANING: Before crested lizard

DATE: Late Cretaceous

GROUP: Ornithopoda

DIET: Plants

SIZE: 26 feet (8 m) long

FOSSIL LOCATIONS: Canada, USA 1916

PRONUNCIATION: PRO-saw-ROL-oh-fus

This duckbill dinosaur is known from several complete skulls and skeletons. It had a solid crest and was closely related to *Saurolophus*. It was one of the first dinosaurs from the Dinosaur Provincial Park, Alberta, Canada, to be named. There are few specimens of this dinosaur, which could mean that it lived in drier areas away from rivers, where skeletons were less likely to be preserved.

Prosaurolophus

Protoceratops

PRONUNCIATION: PRO-toe-SER-a-tops

This Asian ceratopsian is known from hundreds of complete skulls and many skeletons. So many skulls have been found in the Gobi Desert that an entire series, from egg to adult, has been studied. One of the most famous finds is the "fighting dinosaurs." Skeletons of *Protoceratops* and *Velociraptor* have been found locked in combat with *Velocirator*'s arm in *Protoceratops*'s mouth. They were probably fighting on a sand dune that collapsed and killed them mid-battle.

Protoceratops had a well-developed frill that extended back from its face and over its neck. It did not have horns.

Protoceratops had a parrot-like beak that sheared off plants and scissor-like teeth that sliced up its food.

THE FACTS

MEANING:	First horned face
DATE:	Early Cretaceous
GROUP:	Ceratopsia
DIET:	Plants
SIZE:	10 feet (3 m) long
FOSSIL LOCATIONS:	China, Mongolia 1923

☐ *Protoceratops*

FIGHT UNTIL THE END

Velociraptor battles with *Protoceratops*, squashing some dinosaur eggs in the process. This is a recreation of the famous "fighting dinosaurs" fossils—a battle took place about 70 million years ago.

THE FACTS

MEANING: Parrot lizard

DATE: Early Cretaceous

GROUP: Ceratopsia

DIET: Plants

SIZE: 10 feet (3 m) long

FOSSIL LOCATIONS: China, Mongolia, Thailand 1923

Psittacosaurus

PRONUNCIATION: sih-TAK-oh-SAW-rus

This small ceratopsian walked on both two and four legs. It had a parrot-like beak and its teeth could chop plants but not chew them. One adult fossil was found with more than 30 babies in tow. Another specimen, recently found in the famous Yixian Formation in China, had a row of hollow quill-like structures sticking out along the top of its tail. We do not know what these were used for.

Psittacosaurus

THE FACTS

MEANING: Qantas (Australian airline) lizard

DATE: Early Cretaceous

GROUP: Ornithopoda

DIET: Plants

SIZE: 6 feet (2 m) long

FOSSIL LOCATIONS: Australia 1999

Qantassaurus

PRONUNCIATION: KWON-tuh-SAW-rus

This little plant eater lived in Australia about 115 million years ago. As Australia was then in the Antarctic Circle, *Qantassaurus* must have lived a few months each year in "polar night." It had large eyes, probably for night vision. Studies of its bone show that it grew all year, which means that it did not hibernate and was likely to have been warm-blooded. It was named after an airline that was helpful in transporting dinosaur exhibitions at the time.

Qantassaurus

Rugops

PRONUNCIATION: ROO-gops

This abelisaur from Niger, Africa, is noted for the many strong, thick ornamental bones on top of its nose and between its eyes. It also may have had ornamental crests on top of its head. Its skull was wide and short and some scientists think its jaws were too weak for active hunting. It could have eaten the remains of other dead dinosaurs. Its upper jaw curved upward, which probably made *Rugops* look like it was smiling.

THE FACTS

MEANING:	Wrinkle face
DATE:	Late Cretaceous
GROUP:	Theropoda
DIET:	Meat
SIZE:	23–26 feet (7–8 m) long
FOSSIL LOCATIONS:	Niger 2004

Rugops

NEW EVIDENCE

Rugops lived about 95 million years ago. The discovery of a *Rugops* skull in Niger, Africa, demonstrated that this landmass was still a part of the great southern continent, Gondwana, at that stage in Earth's history.

THE FACTS

MEANING: Lizard from Salta (Argentina)

DATE: Late Cretaceous

GROUP: Sauropodamorpha

DIET: Plants

SIZE: 39 feet (12 m) long

FOSSIL LOCATIONS: Argentina 1980

Saltasaurus

PRONUNCIATION: SALT-uh-SAW-rus

This sauropod lived in Argentina near the end of the Cretaceous. It was short and stocky. It had sets of bony lumps in its skin, called dermal ossicles, that lay along each side of its backbone. They ranged from 1 to 8 inches (2.5–20 cm) long—too small to be used as armor but perhaps they were just big enough to break an attacking theropod's teeth.

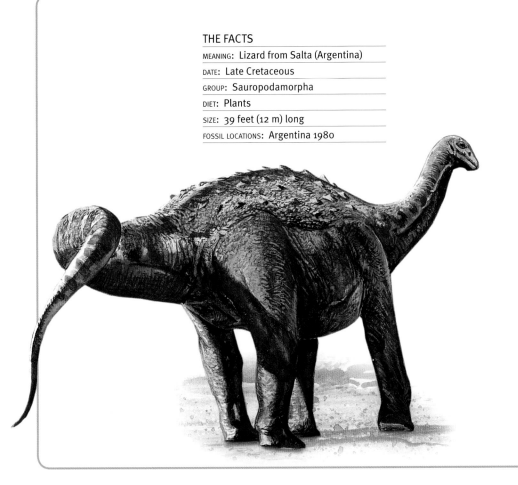

Saltasaurus

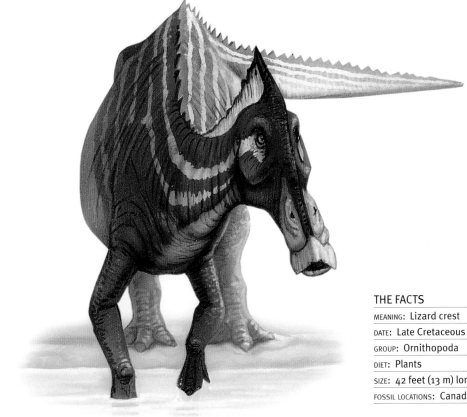

Saurolophus

PRONUNCIATION: SAW-roh-LOW-fus

This duckbill dinosaur could walk on two or four legs. It had a solid crest that projected upward and backward above the top of its head. This crest may have supported a sac of skin on top of its nose, which, when inflated, made a sound like an oboe—this theory can only be tested if a preserved sac is ever found.

THE FACTS

MEANING: Lizard crest

DATE: Late Cretaceous

GROUP: Ornithopoda

DIET: Plants

SIZE: 42 feet (13 m) long

FOSSIL LOCATIONS: Canada, Mongolia 1912

Saurolophus

Scelidosaurus

PRONUNCIATION: SKEL-ee-do-SAW-rus

Scelidosaurus was named by the famous paleontologist, Sir Richard Owen. It was one of the earliest armored dinosaurs to appear on Earth. It had small bony bumps in its skin that lay in parallel rows all the way down its body and tail. Its description was based on a nearly complete skull and skeleton. It was four-legged and its hind legs were longer than it front legs.

THE FACTS

MEANING:	Rib lizard
DATE:	Early Jurassic
GROUP:	Ornithopoda
DIET:	Plants
SIZE:	13 feet (4 m) long
FOSSIL LOCATIONS:	England 1859

Scelidosaurus

Scipionyx

PRONUNCIATION: sip-ee-ON-iks

This young theropod lived in Italy about 110 million years ago. It is one of the best-preserved dinosaurs ever found. This is because it was buried in limestone and in a low-oxygen environment, which prevented the decay that normally occurs during fossilization. The fossil was a rare find—it had preserved soft tissues, including the gut, liver, and muscles.

THE FACTS

MEANING:	For geologist Scipione Breislak
DATE:	Early Cretaceous
GROUP:	Theropoda
DIET:	Meat
SIZE:	6 feet (2 m) long
FOSSIL LOCATIONS:	Italy 1998

Scipionyx

Scutellosaurus

PRONUNCIATION: skoo-TELL-oh-SAW-rus

This small dinosaur was built like an armored ornithischian but it was too primitive to belong to either of the two main groups, the stegosaurs or the ankylosaurs. Its back was covered with bony bumps in the skin, or ossicles. Some were flat and some were raised, like ridges. They were spaced just far enough apart so that a theropod would break at least one tooth if it tried to bite *Scutellosaurus*. This dinosaur walked on two legs, unlike the other armored ornithischians.

THE FACTS

MEANING: Little shield lizard
DATE: Early Jurassic
GROUP: Stegosauria
DIET: Plants
SIZE: 4 feet (1.3 m) long
FOSSIL LOCATIONS: USA 1981

Scutellosaurus

THE FACTS

MEANING: Slow lizard
DATE: Late Cretaceous
GROUP: Theropoda
DIET: Meat
SIZE: 19 feet (6 m) long
FOSSIL LOCATIONS: Mongolia 1979

Segnosaurus

PRONUNCIATION: SEG-noh-SAW-rus

This Cretaceous theropod was one of the therizinosaurs, a group of theropods with a strange mixture of features. *Segnosaurus* had a long skull with small teeth, something like a Triassic prosauropod. Its hands had long claws and its foot had four toes, not three as in most other theropods. These features would make sense if *Segnosaurus* hunted fish from the water—it probably did but we do not know this.

Segnosaurus

Shunosaurus

PRONUNCIATION: SHOO-no-SAW-rus

This Chinese dinosaur was one of the most primitive of the true sauropods. It had both round and spoonlike teeth. Its neck was shorter than the necks of other sauropods. One fossil was so well preserved that the hollow area inside its skull showed the shape of its brain and arteries. So many skeletons have been found at Dashanpu, in China, that a museum has been built over the site. It is China's equivalent of Dinosaur National Park in the USA.

THE FACTS

MEANING: Lizard from Shu (Sichuan, China)
DATE: Late Jurassic
GROUP: Sauropodamorpha
DIET: Plants
SIZE: 33 feet (10 m) long
FOSSIL LOCATIONS: China 1984

Shunosaurus

Shuvuuia

PRONUNCIATION: shu-VOO-ee-a

This tiny, feathered theropod had short arms that were used for digging. Its upper jaw could move independently from the rest of its head, which is a feature found in birds. It ate insects, beetles, termites, and possibly worms. It lived at the same time and in the same place as *Velociraptor*, but they did not compete for food.

THE FACTS

MEANING: Bird (Mongolian dialect)
DATE: Late Cretaceous
GROUP: Theropoda
DIET: Meat
SIZE: 2 feet (60 cm) long
FOSSIL LOCATIONS: Mongolia 1998

Shuvuuia

Sinocalliopteryx

PRONUNCIATION: SY-no-CAL-ee-OP-ter-iks

This Chinese dinosaur was a non-flying feathered theropod that lived in the Cretaceous but belonged to a group that began in the Jurassic. It had no true flight feathers but it had primitive feathers on its ankles. One specimen had the leg of another theropod inside its stomach area. Perhaps this dinosaur ate other smaller, feathered dinosaurs.

Sinocalliopteryx

THE FACTS
MEANING: **Chinese beautiful feather/wing**
DATE: **Early Cretaceous**
GROUP: **Theropoda**
DIET: **Meat**
SIZE: **8 feet (2.4 m) long**
FOSSIL LOCATIONS: **China 2007**

FEATHERED FRIENDS

Sinocalliopteryx was related to *Huaxiagnathus,* a Chinese dinosaur of about half the size. *Sinocalliopteryx* is the longest feathered dinosaur.

Sinornithomimus

PRONUNCIATION: SIGN-or-nith-oh-MIME-us

The description of *Sinornithomimus* is based on the study of nine skeletons of young dinosaurs found together—no adults were found. The nine dinosaurs were probably part of a family group that died at the same time. The adults must have either been away when the disaster hit, or they escaped. Feathers were found with the skeletons, as were stomach stones, or gastroliths, which tell us this dinosaur ate plants.

THE FACTS

MEANING:	Chinese bird mimic
DATE:	Late Cretaceous
GROUP:	Theropoda
DIET:	Meat and plants
SIZE:	6 feet (2 m) long
FOSSIL LOCATIONS:	China, Mongolia 2003

Sinornithomimus

Sinornithosaurus

PRONUNCIATION: SIE-nor-nith-og-SAW-rus

This small predator had many feathers, including downlike tufts, body feathers, and primitive flight feathers. It could flap it arms in the way modern birds do—not all feathered dinosaurs could do this. It also had a sickle claw on each foot. *Sinornithosaurus* was named by the famous Chinese paleontologist, Xu Xing, who has named more feathered dinosaurs than anyone else.

THE FACTS

MEANING:	Chinese bird lizard
DATE:	Early Cretaceous
GROUP:	Theropoda
DIET:	Meat
SIZE:	3 feet (1 m) long
FOSSIL LOCATIONS:	China 1999

Sinornithosaurus

THE FACTS

MEANING: Chinese lizard wing

DATE: Early Cretaceous

GROUP: Theropoda

DIET: Meat

SIZE: 3 feet (1 m) long

FOSSIL LOCATIONS: China 1996

Sinosauropteryx

PRONUNCIATION: SIE-no-saw-ROP-ter-iks

Sinosauropteryx was a feathered Cretaceous theropod. It was the first dinosaur to be named from the famous Liaoning fossil beds in China. It did not have flight feathers, which is unusual because this dinosaur lived tens of millions of years after *Archeopteryx*, from the Jurassic, which did have true flight feathers. One specimen of *Sinosauropteryx* was found with three mammal jaws in its stomach.

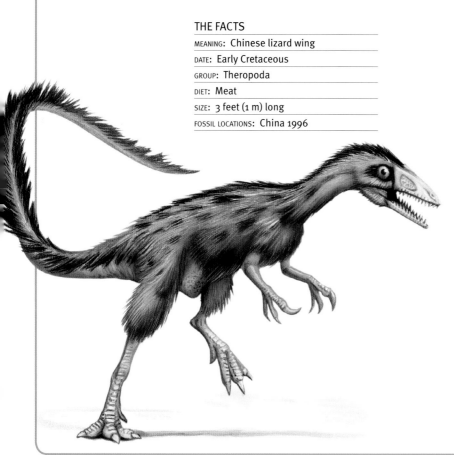

Sinosauropteryx

THE FACTS

MEANING: China hunter

DATE: Lower Cretaceous

GROUP: Theropoda

DIET: Meat

SIZE: 3 feet (1 m) long

FOSSIL LOCATIONS: China 2002

Sinovenator

PRONUNCIATION: SIGH-no-ven-NAY-tor

This was one of the ealiest birdlike dinosaurs, or troodonts. Its legs were much longer than its short arms and it had feathers but it could not fly. Unlike the famous *Troodon*, *Sinovenator* did not have large sawlike bumps on its teeth for tearing flesh. Instead, it had smaller bumps that it used for eating lizards and insects—and perhaps for scavenging.

Sinovenator

Sinraptor

PRONUNCIATION: sien-RAP-tor

This huge Jurassic meat eater was bigger than the well-known theropod *Allosaurus*. One of the first fossils found had teeth marks from another predator, possibly even another *Sinraptor*. These wounds tell us that theropods wrestled using their mouths—with skulls of about 3 feet (1 m) long, these fights would have been dramatic and bloody.

Sinraptor

THE FACTS

MEANING:	China robber
DATE:	Late Jurassic
GROUP:	Theropoda
DIET:	Meat
SIZE:	24 feet (7.2 m) long
FOSSIL LOCATIONS:	China 1993

Sonidosaurus

PRONUNCIATION: SON-id-oh-SAW-rus

Sonidosaurus was a titanosaur from Asia. A titanosaur is from a group of dinosaurs that had bony plates on their skin. *Sonidosaurus* had large, thick spines coming straight up from its backbone. It had a mixture of features from early and later titanosaurs. Some paleontologists think it is an early titanosaur that evolved in Asia, away from the main group of titanosaurs.

THE FACTS

MEANING:	Lizard from Sonid (Mongolia)
DATE:	Late Cretaceous
GROUP:	Sauropodamorpha
DIET:	Plants
SIZE:	29 feet (9 m) long
FOSSIL LOCATIONS:	China 2006

Sonidosaurus

Spinosaurus

Spinosaurus was named for the tall spines that stuck out from its backbone.

PRONUNCIATION: SPY-noh-SAW-rus

This 12-ton (10.8-t) predator was a spinosaur. Spinosaurs were unusual theropods with crocodile-like skulls and a "sail" on their back. The sail probably helped regulate body temperature and was used as a display for mating and territory disputes. The spines along *Spinosaurus*'s back were more than 6 feet (1.8 m) high. It had long hands with long, curved claws. It may have used its claws to hunt fish.

Spinosaurus

THE FACTS

MEANING: Spine lizard

DATE: Early Cretaceous

GROUP: Theropoda

DIET: Meat

SIZE: 33 feet (10 m) long

FOSSIL LOCATIONS: Egypt, North Africa 1915

COOLING DOWN

Spinosaurus was one of the biggest meat-eating dinosaurs ever to have lived. It may have used its sail to help cool down its huge body. It would have stood in the shade when it got too hot and pumped warm blood into the skin on its sail. This blood cooled down before returning to the rest of its body.

Stegosaurus

PRONUNCIATION: STEG-oh-SAW-rus

Stegosaurus is the most famous of all the armored and plated dinosaurs. This dinosaur was designed to defend itself against it main predators, *Allosaurus*, *Ceratosaurus*, and *Torvosaurus*. It had 17 large plates and four tail spikes. It could not outrun its attackers, in fact, it could not run at all, which is why it relied on defense. Even its throat was protected by more than 100 small bones in the skin.

THE FACTS

MEANING:	Roofed lizard
DATE:	Late Jurassic
GROUP:	Stegosauria
DIET:	Plants
SIZE:	29 feet (9 m) long
FOSSIL LOCATIONS:	USA 1877

Stegosaurus

SPIKES AND PLATES

Stegosaurus used the spikes at the end of its tail to swipe at and stab attackers. Its plates were used for protection and may have been used to regulate temperature.

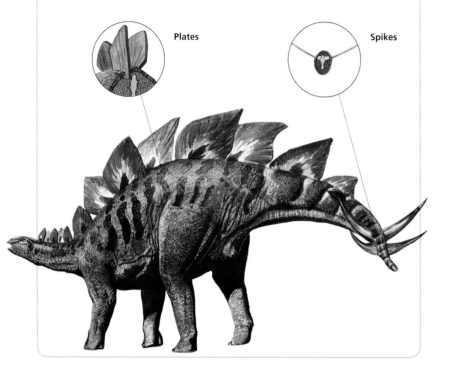

Plates

Spikes

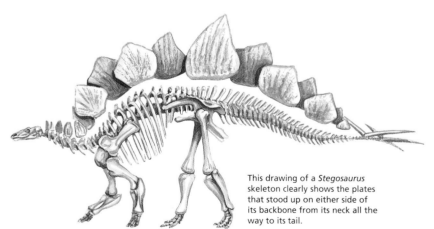

This drawing of a *Stegosaurus* skeleton clearly shows the plates that stood up on either side of its backbone from its neck all the way to its tail.

This skeleton of *Stegosaurus* is in an exhibition at the Royal Tyrrell Museum of Paleontology, Alberta, Canada. Notice how huge its feet are compared to the size of its head.

GIANT PLANT EATER

Stegosaurus had a small head and a long nose. Its teeth were all at the back of its mouth and its upper and lower teeth ground against each other to cut and slice its food. It had a sharp beak at the front of its mouth that was used to cut its food like a pair of shears does. It may have had pouches in its cheeks where it stored food before chewing it.

Struthiomimus

PRONUNCIATION: STROOTH-ee-oh-MY-muss

Struthiomimus was an ostrich-like dinosaur. It had large eyes and long arms with long fingers and it may have had feathers. It had a weak jaw and no teeth but would have been strong enough to eat small prey. *Struthiomimus* was probably an excellent night hunter of small mammals and lizards.

☐ *Struthiomimus*

THE FACTS

MEANING: Ostrich mimic

DATE: Late Cretaceous

GROUP: Theropoda

DIET: Meat

SIZE: 13 feet (4 m) long

FOSSIL LOCATIONS: Canada 1917

Stygimoloch

PRONUNCIATION: STY-gee-MOH-lok

Stygimoloch was a dome-headed dinosaur. Scientists think three dome-headed dinosaurs, *Stygimoloch*, *Dracorex*, and *Pachycephalosaurus* may be different growth stages of the same species, in which the bumps, hooks, and knobs on the skull were gradually replaced by a dome of solid bone. A fully formed dome may have been a way of saying to other dinosaurs, "I am now a mature adult who is strong enough to defend my territory!"

THE FACTS

MEANING: Horned devil from river Styx

DATE: Late Cretaceous

GROUP: Pachycephalosauria

DIET: Plants

SIZE: 20 feet (6 m) long

FOSSIL LOCATIONS: USA 1983

☐ *Stygimoloch*

Styracosaurus

PRONUNCIATION: sty-RACK-oh-SAW-rus

THE FACTS

MEANING: Spiked lizard

DATE: Late Cretaceous

GROUP: Ceratopsia

DIET: Plants

SIZE: 18 feet (5.5 m) long

FOSSIL LOCATIONS: Canada, USA 1913

Styracosaurus

The ceratopsian dinosaurs were divided into two major groups: centrosaurines and chasmosaurines. Centrosaurines had a relatively short frill and their heads were decorated with spikes, knobs, and hooks. The nose horn tended to be larger. Chasmosaurines, which included *Triceratops*, had longer frills and a larger brow horn. *Styracosaurus* was a centrosaurine and had a set of frill spikes, a cheek spike, and a long nose horn. This horn was long enough to pierce right through the leg of a theropod.

DISPLAY OF AGGRESSION

Styracosaurus's nose horn and spiked head shield looked threatening to its attackers. Its spiky frill protected its neck and its huge nose horn could rip open a predator's belly.

Talenkauen

PRONUNCIATION: TAY-len-KOW-en

This ornithopod from Argentina lived at the end of the Cretaceous, but it looked more like a Jurassic ornithopod. It had a series of small, overlapping ¹/₁₀-inch (3-mm) armored plates across its ribs, which were too thin to serve as a defense against predators—unlike ankylosaurs' and stegosaurs' theropod-proof armor. *Talenkauen* had long legs and a light build—its main defense was escape.

☐ *Talenkauen*

THE FACTS

MEANING:	Small skull
DATE:	Late Cretaceous
GROUP:	Ornithopoda
DIET:	Plants
SIZE:	13 feet (4 m) long
FOSSIL LOCATIONS:	Argentina 2004

Tazoudasaurus

PRONUNCIATION: tah-ZOO-dah-SAW-rus

Tazoudasaurus had a mixture of prosauropod and true sauropod features. Its teeth had small bumps, or serrations, that helped it tear up its food. Serrated teeth were almost unknown in other sauropods, who normally swallowed their food whole. This makes *Tazoudasaurus* the most primitive true sauropod so far discovered.

THE FACTS

MEANING:	Lizard from Tazouda (Morocco)
DATE:	Early Jurassic
GROUP:	Sauropodamorpha
DIET:	Plants
SIZE:	30 feet (9 m) long
FOSSIL LOCATIONS:	Morocco 2004

☐ *Tazoudasaurus*

THE FACTS

MEANING: Sinew lizard

DATE: Early Cretaceous

GROUP: Ornithopoda

DIET: Plants

SIZE: 26 feet (8 m) long

FOSSIL LOCATIONS: USA 1970

Tenontosaurus

PRONUNCIATION: ten-ON-toh-SAW-rus

This ornithopod is most famous for being the prey of *Deinonychus*. At one site, a body of *Tenontosaurus* was found with two *Deinonychus* skeletons nearby. Scientists think *Deinonychus* killed and partially ate the plant eater and the two other *Deinonychus* were then attracted to the free meal. After a fight over the body, the two *Deinonychus* were killed. The bones of *Tenontosaurus* showed tooth marks that look like *Deinonychus* teeth impressions.

Tenontosaurus

THE FACTS

MEANING: Bull lizard

DATE: Late Cretaceous

GROUP: Ceratopsia

DIET: Plants

SIZE: 25 feet (7.5 m) long

FOSSIL LOCATIONS: Canada, USA 1891

Torosaurus

PRONUNCIATION: TOR-oh-SAW-rus

Torosaurus had one of the longest skulls ever found, it was 10 feet (3 m) long. The frill was more than half the length of the skull and had two large openings to make it lighter. Its skull and body were more lightly built than those of the massive *Triceratops*, the most famous ceratopsian. Both dinosaurs lived to the end of the Cretaceous, but there were not so many *Torosaurus*. For every one *Torosaurus* skull found, 15 *Triceratops* skulls were found.

Torosaurus

Triceratops

PRONUNCIATION: try-SER-a-tops

This famous dinosaur was one of the last dinosaurs to live on Earth. *Triceratops* is also famous for being a food source for *Tyrannosaurus rex*. Its frill counterbalanced the weight of its head, which was where its massive jaw muscles attached. It had the strongest jaws of any plant eater. Its teeth sharpened themselves on their food and were replaced throughout its life. They sheared past each other like giant shears. *Triceratops* could chomp its way through any vegetation. Although it looked like a rhinoceros, it could not gallop like one. It was much slower than *T. rex* and had to rely on its huge horns for defense.

This fossil skeleton of *Triceratops* clearly shows its frill of solid bone and its three horns. The frill covered the dinosaur's soft neck to protect it from attack.

☐ *Triceratops*

THE FACTS

MEANING:	Three-horned face
DATE:	Late Cretaceous
GROUP:	Ceratopsia
DIET:	Plants
SIZE:	30 feet (9 m) long
FOSSIL LOCATIONS:	Canada, USA 1889

TRICERATOPS HORNS AND FRILL

Triceratops's two horns above its eyes grew to more than 3 feet (1 m) long. The horn on its nose was smaller. *Triceratops*'s frill could have been used for courtship display and temperature regulation.

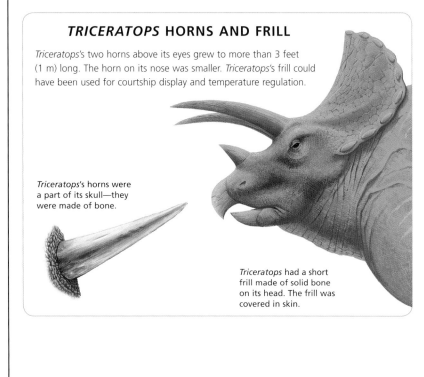

Triceratops's horns were a part of its skull—they were made of bone.

Triceratops had a short frill made of solid bone on its head. The frill was covered in skin.

A SURVIVOR

Although *Triceratops* lived when there were many fierce theropods, including *Tyrannosaurus*, it survived until the end of the Cretaceous. It used its three horns to charge and stab its attackers and it used its frill to protect its neck from predators' teeth.

Troodon

PRONUNCIATION: TROH-o-don

This theropod had many unique features. Its brain was one of the largest of any dinosaur, relative to its size, which means it was probably one of the smartest dinosaurs. It had stereoscopic vision so it had good depth perception, and it had big eyes. Its teeth had large serrations—they resembled the teeth of some of the plant-eating prosauropods, which could mean *Troodon* ate plants and animals. *Troodon* was one of the first dinosaurs to be named in the USA.

THE FACTS

MEANING: Wounding tooth

DATE: Late Cretaceous

GROUP: Theropoda

DIET: Meat

SIZE: 10 feet (3 m) long

FOSSIL LOCATIONS: Canada, USA 1856

Troodon

Tuojiangosaurus

PRONUNCIATION: toh-HWANG-oh-SAW-rus

Tuojiangosaurus looked just like a *Stegosaurus* ancestor should look. Both dinosaurs had armor plates and tail spikes but *Tuojiangosaurus*'s plates were smaller and more pointed. Unlike *Stegosaurus*, it had a large spike sticking out from its shoulder. This is one of the best-known stegosaurs from China—there have been so many stegosaurs found here that scientists think Asia may have been where this group of dinosaurs first appeared.

THE FACTS

MEANING: Lizard from Tuo River (China)

DATE: Late Jurassic

GROUP: Stegosauria

DIET: Plants

SIZE: 23 feet (7 m) long

FOSSIL LOCATIONS: China 1977

Tuojiangosaurus

THE FACTS

MEANING: Lizard from Teruel

DATE: Jurassic–Cretaceous boundary

GROUP: Sauropodamorpha

DIET: Plants

SIZE: 98–121 feet (30–37 m) long

FOSSIL LOCATIONS: Spain 2006

Turiasaurus

Turiasaurus

PRONUNCIATION: TUR-ee-ah-SAW-rus

This may be the largest dinosaur from Europe ever found. The upper arm bone of the skelton is 70 inches (1.8 m) long and the huge big-toe claw on its hind foot is the size of a football. It belongs to a new group of sauropods and probably evolved separately from the more famous *Diplodocus* and *Brachiosaurus*.

BIG BUT NOT THE BIGGEST

Turiasaurus probably weighed as much as eight fully grown African elephants. It may be the largest European sauropod but it is not as big as the American and African giants.

Tyrannosaurus

PRONUNCIATION: tie-RAN-oh-SAW-rus

Tyrannosaurus rex is the most famous dinosaur of all time. It lived at the end of the Cretaceous and dined on *Triceratops* and *Edmontosaurus*. There have been two other contenders for the title of "largest land predator of all time"—*Carcharodontosaurus* and *Giganotosaurus*. However, *T. rex* had a larger and more powerful skull. Its teeth were thicker and longer—they grew more than 5 inches (14 cm) above the gum line. Both sides of each tooth had serrations, similar to a saw's. *T. rex* could gulp down 44 pounds (20 kg) of meat in one swallow. It is hard to tell whether *T. rex* was a predator or a scavenger but it was probably both.

THE FACTS

MEANING:	Tyrant lizard
DATE:	Late Cretaceous
GROUP:	Theropoda
DIET:	Meat
SIZE:	40 feet (12 m) long
FOSSIL LOCATIONS:	Canada, USA 1905

TYRANNOSAURUS SKULL

The skull of *Tyrannosaurus* was powerful enough to crunch down and kill its prey. Its heavy jaw had an extra joint in the middle, so the mouth could open wide to take extra-large bites. It had bony bits above and below its eyes to protect them from being damaged by struggling prey.

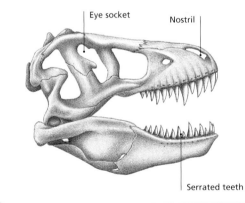

Eye socket

Nostril

Serrated teeth

MIGHTY HUNTER

Tyrannosaurus had good eyesight, a strong jaw, and powerful legs. It's arms, however, were small and it had two-fingered, clawed hands. *Tyrannosaurus* survived by scavenging and by actively hunting prey. Here it is feasting on the carcass of a dead plant eater, *Edmontosaurus*.

This huge *Tyrannosaurus* thighbone is part of a nearly complete skeleton found in the USA. The complete skeleton will be mounted in a museum exhibition.

Tyrannosaurus

Unaysaurus

PRONUNCIATION: yoo-NAH-ee-SAW-rus

This small, 165-pound (75-kg) prosauropod came from Brazil. It is one of the earliest known dinosaurs. *Unaysaurus* lived in the Triassic when all the landmasses were connected to form the supercontinent Pangea. It was closely related to *Plateosaurus*, the first giant sauropod, which lived in what is now Europe—at the end of the Triassic it was possible to walk from Brazil to Germany.

OLD BUT WELL PRESERVED

Unaysaurus's fossil is well preserved, even though this is one of the world's oldest known dinosaurs. The fossil is incomplete but it is still one of the most complete skeletons ever found and many bones are still in their original positions.

Unaysaurus

THE FACTS

MEANING: Black water lizard

DATE: Late Triassic

GROUP: Sauropodamorpha

DIET: Plants

SIZE: 8 feet (2.5 m) long

FOSSIL LOCATIONS: Brazil 2004

Utahraptor

PRONUNCIATION: YOO-tah-RAP-tor

Utahraptor

Utahraptor was a giant dromaeosaur, or birdlike theropod. It had a 9-inch (23-cm) sickle claw on each foot, which was its main weapon of attack. It weighed 1,543 pounds (700 kg) and was fast enough to catch anything smaller than itself. Like other dromaeosaurs, it probably had feathers on its body and arms.

THE FACTS

MEANING: **Thief from Utah**

DATE: **Early Cretaceous**

GROUP: **Theropoda**

DIET: **Meat**

SIZE: **20–23 feet (6–7 m) long**

FOSSIL LOCATIONS: **USA 1993**

MIGHTY PREDATOR

Utahraptor's claws could have been used for stabbing or slashing its prey—some scientists believe they could have also been used for suffocating.

Velociraptor

PRONUNCIATION: ve-LOSS-i-RAP-tor

Velociraptor was a lightly built, fast predator with a deadly sickle-shaped claw on each foot. Its relatively large brain size tells us that it must have been one of the smartest dinosaurs. It is also one of the most famous. In the Gobi Desert, in 1971, a complete skeleton was found locked in a death grip with *Protoceratops*. These two dinosaurs have been fighting for more than 75 million years.

☐ Velociraptor

THE FACTS

MEANING:	Rapid thief
DATE:	Late Cretaceous
GROUP:	Theropoda
DIET:	Meat
SIZE:	3 feet (1 m) long
FOSSIL LOCATIONS:	Mongolia, China 1924

Velociraptor had a large brain for its body size. The only smarter dinosaur that we know of is *Troodon*.

BUMPS ON A WING

Velociraptor was a two-legged, feathered dinosaur. We know it had feathers because scientists recently found knobs on a *Velociraptor*'s forearm that were the same as the bumps on bird wingbones where their feathers were connected.

THE FACTS

MEANING: Lizard from Wuerho (China)

DATE: Early Cretaceous

GROUP: Stegosauria

DIET: Plants

SIZE: 19 feet (6 m) long

FOSSIL LOCATIONS: China 1973

Wuerhosaurus

PRONUNCIATION: WHERE-oh-SAW-rus

This armored Cretaceous dinosaur may have been one of the last stegosaurs to live, as most known stegosaurs were Jurassic. Like its American cousin, *Stegosaurus*, it had four spikes on the end of its tail and a series of plates along its backbone. However, these plates were longer and lower than the tall, triangular ones of *Stegosaurus.* Its also held its head lower to the ground.

Wuerhosaurus

THE FACTS

MEANING: Hidden dragon

DATE: Late Jurassic

GROUP: Theropoda

DIET: Meat

SIZE: 3 feet (1 m) long

FOSSIL LOCATIONS: China 2006

Yinlong

Yinlong

PRONUNCIATION: yin-LONG

Yinlong is the only known Jurassic ceratopsian—all other ceratopsians were Cretaceous. It had bony projections on the back of its skull that looked like those in the pachycephalosaurs, or the "boneheads." It had an upper beak bone, which was a feature of all ceratopsians, and two "fangs." These features are very unusual in a Jurassic dinosaur.

Comparisons

AN AVERAGE DINOSAUR

When we think "dinosaurs" we usually think "big." But a large majority of dinosaurs were nowhere near as big as the giants *Seismosaurus* or *Giganotosaurus*. Most were small, like *Velociraptor*, which was about the size of a basset hound.

Basset hound
4 feet (1.2 m) long
2 feet (0.6 m) tall

Velociraptor
6 feet (1.8 m) long
2 feet (0.6 m) tall

PLANT EATERS AND MEAT EATERS

Paleontologists can determine what dinosaurs ate by studying their fossils. Of all the dinosaur fossils found, about 65 percent are plant eaters. Scientists believe that if we knew of every dinosaur that ever lived, the proportion of plant eaters to meat eaters would be even greater. Meat eaters ate plant-eating dinosaurs, small mammals, lizards, or insects. Plant eaters ate cycads, tree ferns, leaves, or seeds—whatever they could reach, swallow, and digest.

Plant-eating dinosaurs 65%   Meat-eating dinosaurs 35%

FIERCE CLAWS

The longest dinosaur claws belonged to *Therizinosaurus*, but the claws on *Deinonychus*'s back feet were about the same size as that of a modern harpy eagle.

Modern harpy eagle
Claws 5 inches (13 cm) long

THE HEAVYWEIGHTS

The African elephant is the heaviest land animal alive today. It is heavier than many small dinosaurs and probably weighed about the same as *Tyrannosaurus*. It outweighed *Protoceratops* 15 to one. However, an elephant is only a fraction of the size of giant plant-eating dinosaurs such as *Argentinosaurus*.

15 *Protoceratops*
880 pounds
(400 kg) each =

1 African elephant
6.5 tons (6 t)

1 *Tyrannosaurus*
6.5 tons (6 t) =

1 African elephant
6.5 tons (6 t)

1 *Argentinosaurus*
110.5 tons (100 t) =

17 African elephants
6.5 tons (6 t) each

Therizinosaurus
Claws 36 inches (91 cm) long

Deinonychus
Claws 5 inches (13 cm) long

LONGEST DINOSAUR
ARGENTINOSAURUS
150 feet (45 m) long and
18 feet (5.5 m) tall at shoulder

BIG AND SMALL

Giganotosaurus was the biggest meat-eater, so far. The longest was *Argentinosaurus*, so far. Most were much smaller. The smallest dinosaur found was one that just hatched from its egg.

LARGEST MEAT EATER
GIGANOTOSAURUS
47 feet (14 m) long and
12 feet (3.6 m) tall at the shoulder

MODERN GIRAFFE
18 feet (5.5 m) tall

MODERN BOY
4.5 feet (1.4 m) tall

Paleontology

IN THE FIELD

A paleontologist studies ancient life using fossils. Fossils are the preserved remains of plants or animals that turned to stone or left their impression on rock. Sometimes whole skeletons are fossilized.

COULD DINOSAURS COME BACK?

Dinosaurs are often shown in movies as living at the same time as humans. We know this did not happen in reality, but could they come back to life today? The answer is no. In the movie *Jurassic Park*, scientists brought the dinosaurs back to life with a technique called genetic engineering. But to use it, you need dinosaur DNA. We do not have any complete dinosaur DNA and probably never will.

FOSSIL EVIDENCE

Layers of rock have been laid down since the beginning of Earth's history. Before mountain-building begins, the deepest rock is the oldest, that is, it was the first to be laid down. This means the deepest layers, from a time earlier in Earth's history, contain little fossil material. As the layers get closer to the surface, from later in Earth's history, scientists find more complex fossils and sometimes whole skeletons.

CLEANING FOSSILS

Dinosaur bones must be cleaned, repaired, and studied before scientists can reconstruct and display a dinosaur skeleton. Technicians take many hours to do this in the laboratory. They have to be extemely careful not to damage the bones.

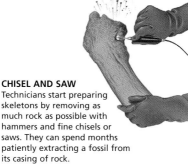

CHISEL AND SAW
Technicians start preparing skeletons by removing as much rock as possible with hammers and fine chisels or saws. They can spend months patiently extracting a fossil from its casing of rock.

BLASTING
If the fossil bone is very hard, technicians can shoot blasts of tiny pieces of sand to erode the rock away. Sometimes the fossil is dipped in acid, which dissolves the surrounding rock.

PRESERVATION
Technicians apply special glues and plastics to the fossil to make sure it will not fall apart—this will preserve the bones forever.

FINE FINISH
To remove the last bits of rock or to work on a fine fossil, technicians need a microscope. They may use an air-powered engraver, a scalpel, a dentist's drill—even a pin held in a hand vice—to finish the job.

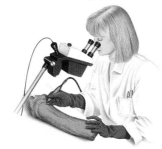

HOW TO SPEAK LIKE A PALEONTOLOGIST

Do you know the difference between the following words? *Tyrannosaurus*, tyrannosaurid, tyrannosauroid, Tyrannosauridae, Tyrannosauroidea? Paleontologists use special endings on names to indicate what types of names they are and their importance. These endings are based on Latin and ancient Greek words. There are international rules about how dinosaur names are used.

All scientific names have two parts, the **genus** and the **species**. Each genus contains one or more species. *Tyrannosaurus* is a genus name and *Tyrannosaurus rex* is one of its species. The genus name is always capitalized, while the species name is never capitalized. Closely related genera—more than one genus— are grouped into families.

Tyrannosaurus is a member of the family Tyrannosauridae. Family names are always capitalized because they are proper names, or nouns, in the same way that your last name is capitalized. Notice that the family name ends in "idae." This is the special ending that means that it is a family name.

When the family name is used to describe a dinosaur, the ending is changed to 'id', and the name is not capitalized.

Now you can use the following sentences in conversation: *Tyrannosaurus rex* is a kind of *Tyrannosaurus*. *Tyrannosaurus* is a member of the family Tyrannosauridae. *Albertosaurus* and *Gorgosaurus* are also tyrannosaurids.

Smithsonian Institution

WASHINGTON DC, UNITED STATES OF AMERICA

The Smithsonian Institution is the world's largest museum complex and research organization. It has 19 museums and nine research centers. Its National Museum of Natural History contains almost 50 million fossils. Its dinosaur collection includes more than 1,500 fossils. The collection includes late Jurassic dinosaurs, such as *Allosaurus*, *Stegosaurus*, *Ceratosaurus*, and *Diplodocus*. It has permanent exhibitions that include mounted dinosaur skeletons, including *Albertosaurus*, *Allosaurus*, *Camarasaurus*, *Diplodocus*, *Ceratosaurus*, *Corythosaurus*, *Edmontosaurus*, *Stegosaurus*, and *Triceratops*—as well as mounted casts of the skeletons of a baby *Maiasaura* and the small South African dinosaur *Heterodontosaurus*. There is also a FossiLab where you can watch paleontologists at work cleaning fossils and making casts and molds.

Tyrannosaurus exhibit

Smithsonian Institution

ON DISPLAY

Late Cretaceous theropods, hadrosaurs, and neoceratopsians, and late Jurassic dinosaurs from the Morrison Formation in Wyoming.

www.mnh.si.edu

American Museum of Natural History

NEW YORK, UNITED STATES OF AMERICA

The American Museum of Natural History (AMNH), in New York City, was first incorporated in 1869. Now the largest private museum in the world, AMNH houses a large collection of dinosaur specimens, including the largest collection of real dinosaur material anywhere in the world. It is also is a major research center for work on dinosaur systematics and evolution. The AMNH's Halls of Saurischian and Ornithischian Dinosaurs, which were completed in the mid-1990s, display more than 100 dinosaur specimens. About 85 percent of these—including the famous skeletons of *Tyrannosaurus*, *Apatosaurus*, *Triceratops*, and *Euoplocephalus*—consist entirely of original material.

The main entrance

ON DISPLAY

A wide range of dinosaur exhibits, both saurischian and ornithischian. Spectacular skeletons include *Tyrannosaurus*, *Diplodocus*, *Triceratops*, and *Euoplocephalus*.

www.amnh.org

American Museum of Natural History

Natural History Museum

The Natural History Museum

LONDON, UNITED KINGDOM

For 200 years London's Natural History Museum has housed the first dinosaur fossils ever found. It has built up a huge collection of fossils from around the world. The Natural History Museum is well known as a center for research in paleontology, including the study of dinosaurs. Its dinosaur collections contain fossils of *Megalosaurus*, *Baryonyx*, *Cetiosauriscus*, *Hylaeosaurus*, *Hypsilophodon*, *Dacentrurus*, *Rhabdodon*, *Polacanthus*, *Euoplocephalus*, *Thecodontosaurus*, and *Brachiosaurus*. The dinosaur gallery includes mounted skeletons of *Tyrannosaurus rex* and *Triceratops*, plus a model of a *Maiasaura* nest, which inludes hatchlings.

ON DISPLAY

A huge range of dinosaurs from around the world. Most interesting are *Euoplocephalus, Diplodocus, Triceratops, Iguanodon, Baryonyx, Hypsilophodon, Brachiosaurus, Archaeopteryx,* and *Scelidosaurus.*

www.nhm.ac.uk

Natural History Museum

Musée National d'Histoire Naturelle

La Galérie de Palinto

PARIS, FRANCE

The Institut de Paléontologie (The Institute of Paloeontology) is part of France's Musée National d'Histoire Naturelle (France's National Museum of Natural History). The museum houses the large anatomy collection of a famous French anatomist Baron Georges Cuvier (1769–1832), and also has many fossils from around the world. It has dinosaur fossils from France, Africa, and parts of South-East Asia. Triassic dinosaurs in the institute include the prosauropod *Plateosaurus* and Moroccan specimens of *Azendohsaurus*. The most complete Jurassic dinosaur known from France is a small skeleton of the little theropod *Compsognathus corallestris*.

ON DISPLAY

Displays include *Iguanodon, Allosaurus, Diplodocus, Tyrannosaurus,* and *Tarbosaurus.*

www.mnhn.fr

Musée National d'Histoire Naturelle

Glossary

abelisaurids A group of large, two-legged, meat-eating dinosaurs that lived in Gondwana during the Cretaceous. They were the equivalent of the tyrannosaurs in Laurasia.

angiosperm All flowering plants, such as grasses, magnolias, and lilies.

ankylosaurids A group of plant-eating dinosaurs, such as *Euoplocephalus*, that lived worldwide. They were heavily armored with thick plates of bone, spikes, and bony skin. They had thick skulls and clubs of solid bone on their tails.

archosaurs A major group of reptiles, which includes the living crocodiles and alligators, as well as the extinct dinosaurs and pterosaurs, and their close relatives.

articulated bones Bones that are arranged in their correct place in the skeleton.

bacteria Microscopic life that was one of the first life forms on Earth.

badlands The landscape where many dinosaur fossils are found. Badlands are often remote, dry, and barren areas where rivers and wind have eroded layers of rock to reveal fossils. There are badlands in Montana, Utah, Wyoming, Colorado, and New Mexico in the United States; in Alberta in Canada; in Patagonia in South America; and in the Gobi Desert in China and Mongolia.

bipedal Walking on two legs.

bone bed A layer of rock full of fossil bones. A famous bone bed can be found at Dinosaur Provincial Park in Canada.

braincase The part of a skull that surrounds and protects the brain. Dinosaur brains are rarely preserved, but paleontologists can work out the size of the brain by examining the braincase.

camouflage A way of disguising something so that it blends with, or remains hidden in, its environment. Some dinosaurs' skin may have been the same color as their environment to camouflage them from prey or other predators.

canyon A deep, steep-sided valley formed by river erosion.

carnivore An animal that eats meat.

carnosaurs A primitive group of non-feathered, massive, powerful, meat-eating theropod dinosaurs, such as *Allosaurus* and *Giganotosaurus*. They were predators as well as scavengers.

cartilage A soft, rubbery substance that separates bones and can develop into bone as the skeleton matures. Cartilage is rarely fossilized.

cast An exact replica of a fossil bone or skeleton made in plastic, plaster, or resin. Soft tissue may also be preserved as fossil casts in stone.

Cenozoic era This era began with the extinction of the dinosaurs 65 million years ago and continues on to today. It is known as the Age of Mammals.

cephalopod A group of soft-bodied animals related to snails that mostly enclose themselves inside hard shells. Cephalopods include ammonites, squid, cuttlefish, and octopuses.

ceratopsians A group of four-legged plant-eating dinosaurs, such as *Triceratops*. Their large heads had horns and bony neck frills. They were one of the last groups of dinosaurs to evolve and traveled in huge herds, browsing over the plains of North America and Asia for 20 million years.

ceratosaurs Medium-size Jurassic theropod dinosaurs distinguished by the small crests or bony horns on their noses. Trackways made by *Ceratosaurus* indicated that these predators may have hunted in packs to bring down larger dinosaurs.

climate A region's long-term pattern of weather conditions.

coal A sedimentary rock formed by the compression of plant remains and sediment layers. It can be burned for fuel.

coelurosaurs The largest group of the meat-eating dinosaurs. They were most common during the Cretaceous period and birds evolved from them. All feathered dinosaurs and *Tyrannosaurus*, are in this group.

"cold-blooded" An outdated term for animals such as snakes and lizards. "Cold-blooded" means they get their body heat from the outside environment, by sitting in the sun. On a cold day they are less active.

conifer A tree with hard, needle-like leaves that holds its seed within cones. Pine trees are conifers.

continent A large area of continental crust with a surface that is above sea level. There are seven continents: Africa, Antarctica, Asia, Australia, Europe, North America, South American.

coprolite Fossilized feces. A dropping that has become a fossil.

Cretaceous period The third and last geological period of the Mesozoic era, when many dinosaurs evolved, then became extinct. It lasted from 144 to 65 million years ago.

crocodilians The only living archosaur reptiles. They include crocodiles, alligators, and caimans.

cycad A primitive, palmlike tree that flourished in the Triassic and Jurassic. Cycads had hard, woody stems with large, frondlike leaves, and reproduced by seeds in cones. Only a few species survive today and all of them are poisonous to mammals.

dromaeosaurs A group of birdlike dinosaurs with slashing claws, which includes *Velociraptor*. They are the dinosaur group closest to the origin of birds.

ecosystem An interdependent community of plants, animals, and other organisms, and the environment in which they live; for example, wetland, desert, pond, or coral reef.

era A division of time in Earth's history. Geologists divide eras into periods.

erosion The wearing away of Earth's surface by rivers, rain, waves, glaciers, or winds.

evolution The gradual changing of plants and animals over millions of years. Dinosaurs evolved from their ancestors, then into different species during the Mesozoic era.

excavation Uncovering something, then digging it out of the ground. Any kind of fossil has to be excavated carefully.

extinction The dying out of a species, or of large communities of animals and plants (called a mass extinction). Mesozoic dinosaurs became extinct at the end of the Cretaceous. Their descendents, the birds, did not.

fossil The preserved remains or traces of plants or animals. These were buried and then turned to stone or left their impression on rock.

gastroliths Stomach or gizzard stones. Some dinosaurs swallowed these stones to help digest the food in their stomachs.

genus A group of closely related species.

geological time The vast length of time that stretches from the formation of Earth to the present day. Geological time is divided into eons, then eras, then periods, epoch, and stages.

geologist A person who studies geology or is involved in the exploration of Earth for economic rocks and minerals.

geology The study of Earth. Rocks, minerals and fossils give some clues to Earth's history.

Gondwana The southern supercontinent formed when Pangea split into two, a process that began about 240 million years ago. It included present-day Africa, Antarctica, Australia, India, Madagascar, and South America.

hadrosaurs Duck-billed, plant-eating dinosaurs, such as *Parasaurolophus*. They had broad, ducklike beaks, batteries of grinding teeth, and many had bony head crests. They evolved in Asia during the early Cretaceous, before spreading to Europe and the Americas. They were the most common and varied ornithopods of the period.

herbivore An animal that eats only plants.

heterodontosaurs An early Jurassic group of ornithopod dinosaurs mostly from southern Africa. They may be the ancestors of the ceratopsians.

horsetail fern Primitive, swamp-living plants related to ferns. Horsetail ferns once grew as large as modern tree ferns, but only a few small species survive today.

hypsilophodontids A group of small two-legged, plant-eating dinosaurs, most common in the Cretaceous.

ichthyosaurs A group of dolphin-like marine reptiles that lived at the same time as the dinosaurs. They gave birth to live young in the sea.

iguanodontians Large, plant-eating ornithopod dinosaurs, such as *Iguanodon*, that mostly walked on four feet. They first appeared during the Jurassic period and became widespread during the early Cretaceous period.

ilium The main bone of the pelvis. The ilium supports the legs and is attached to the backbone.

invertebrate An animal, such as a worm, mollusk, trilobite, or insect, that does not have a backbone.

ischium One of the bones of the pelvis. In dinosaurs, the ischium pointed downward and backward, and supported the muscles of the legs and tail.

Jurassic period The middle geological period of the Mesozoic era. It lasted from 208 to 144 million years ago. The conditions on Earth were just right for new kinds of dinosaurs to flourish, particularly the huge, long-necked sauropods.

Laurasia The northern supercontinent formed when Pangea split into two. It included present-day Europe, North America, and most of Asia.

mammals A group of backboned animals that have hair or fur and feed their young on milk. Humans are mammals, as are dogs, cats, and bats.

marginocephalians A group of ornithischian dinosaurs featuring bony growths along the margin of the head. This group includes the ceratopsians and pachycephalosaurs.

matrix The rock still attached to a fossil after it has been dug out of the ground. The matrix is carefully removed from around the fossil by skilled technicians in the laboratory.

Mesozoic era The Age of Dinosaurs. It began about 250 million years ago, before dinosaurs had evolved, and ended about 65 million years ago with a mass extinction of plants and animals. It spanned the Triassic, Jurassic, and Cretaceous periods.

metatarsal One of the long bones behind the toes in the foot.

meteor A streak of light in the night sky caused by a lump of rock entering Earth's atmosphere from space. Before the rock enters the atmosphere it is known as a meteoroid. If it lands on Earth's surface, it is called a meteorite.

meteorite A mass of rock or metal that has fallen to Earth from a meteor in outerspace.

migration A number of animals moving from one region to another, perhaps to breed or to find food during winter or summer. Hadrosaurs and ceratopsians migrated across North America in herds.

mineral A naturally formed solid with an ordered arrangement of atoms found in Earth's crust that is not a plant or animal.

mosasaurs An extinct group of large marine lizards also known as

"sea dragons." They lived in inshore waters during the Late Cretaceous. They had thick, eel-shaped bodies with four flippers.

mummified Dried out by heat or wind. Some dinosaurs were preserved in this way, before being buried in a sandstorm or volcanic ash. Even their skin and organs may have been fossilized.

nodosaurids One of the two main groups of ankylosaurs. This group does not have the bony club at the end of its tail.

omnivore An animal that eats both prey animals and plant matter.

ornithischians "Bird-hipped" dinosaurs. In this group, the pubis pointed back and down, parallel to the ischium. All the ornithischian dinosaurs were plant eaters.

ornithomimosaur A group of speedy, ostrich-like theropod dinosaurs, such as *Gallimimus*.

ornithopods "Bird-footed," two-legged ornithischian dinosaurs. This group included the hadrosaurs, and iguanodontians.

pachycephalosaurs The "boneheads," a group of plant-eating dinosaurs with skulls thickened into domes of bone. Most lived during the late Cretaceous period in North America and Asia.

paleontologist A scientist who studies ancient life, especially the fossils of plants and animals.

Paleozoic era The Age of Ancient Life, before the Mesozoic. It consists of six periods: Cambrian, Ordovician, Silurian, Devonian, Carboniferous, and Permian. It began 540 million years ago with an explosion of life in the Cambrian, and ended 245 million years ago with a devastating extinction event at the end of the Permian.

Pangea The supercontinent linking all the modern continents. It formed in the Permian period and started to break up during the Triassic.

period A standard division of time in Earth's history that is shorter than an era.

petrified Bone, or other types of organic matter, that has had its layers replaced by minerals.

plesiosaurs Large, fish-eating marine reptiles that flourished during the Jurassic and Cretaceous. Their long necks could

rise above the sea's surface. They swam through the water using their four paddle-like flippers.

pliosaurs A group of marine reptiles that had large heads with strong teeth, short necks, and sturdy, streamlined bodies. They were one of the largest killers of the Mesozoic seas.

predator An animal that hunts or preys on other animals for its food.

prey Animals that predators catch to eat.

prosauropods The first group of the giant sauropods to appear. These plant eaters, such as *Plateosaurus*, lived from the late Triassic to the early Jurassic.

pterosaurs Flying reptiles, only distantly related to dinosaurs. Pterosaurs evolved during the late Triassic period, and had wingspans ranging from 1 foot (30 cm) to 45 feet (14 m).

pubis One of the lower bones of the pelvis. In saurischian dinosaurs it pointed forward; in ornithischians it lay parallel to the ischium and pointed backward.

quadrupedal Walking on four legs.

reptiles A group of backboned animals. They have scaly skin and their young hatch out of shelled eggs. Snakes, lizards, and crocodiles are modern reptiles.

saurischians "Lizard-hipped" dinosaurs, with the pubis pointed forward toward the belly. Two-legged, meat-eating theropods and four-legged, plant-eating sauropods were both saurischians.

sauropods A group of four-legged saurischian dinosaurs with long necks and tails, such as *Diplodocus*. They had lizard-like hips, while most other plant eaters had birdlike hips. Evolving in the late Triassic, they included the largest animals ever to walk on Earth.

scavenger A meat-eating animal that feeds on dead animals or carcasses. It either waits until the hunter has eaten its fill or it steals the dead animal from the hunter.

serrated teeth Teeth that have sawlike edges. Many theropods had serrated teeth to tear through flesh.

species A group of animals or plants that can breed with each other and produce young that can also breed. A group of similar species forms a

genus. *Tyrannosaurus rex* was a species of the *Tyrannosaurus* genus of dinosaurs.

spinosaurs A group of "sail-backed" Cretaceous theropod dinosaurs with enlarged thumb-claws and long, thin, crocodile-like snouts. They were most abundant in Gondwana.

stegosaurs Four-legged, plant-eating dinosaurs with bony plates along their backs and long, sharp spikes on their strong tails. From the late Jurassic period, they roamed North America, Europe, Asia, and Africa, and included *Stegosaurus*.

synapsids A group of animals that appeared along with the reptiles. Synapsids lived before the dinosaurs and mammals evolved from them.

therizinosaurs A group of unusual dinosaurs that were theropods but had some features similar to prosauropods. They included *Segnosaurus* and lived during the Cretaceous period.

theropods All the meat-eating dinosaurs. They were lizard-hipped and walked on their back legs.

trackways A series of footprints left by an animal walking or running over soft ground. Sometimes, dinosaur trackways became fossilized.

Triassic period The first geological period in the Mesozoic era, from 245 to 208 million years ago. Dinosaurs appeared about halfway through this period, around 228 million years ago.

trilobite Small crablike creatures with three body parts that lived in the seas of the Paleozoic era. Trilobites became extinct at the end of the Permian, just before the Age of Dinosaurs.

tyrannosaurs A group of theropod dinosaurs such as *Albertosaurus*. They are all related to the last member of their group, *Tyrannosaurus*.

vertebrae The bones along the spine, from the base of the skull to the tail. They protect the spinal column.

vertebrate An animal that has a backbone. Mammals, birds, reptiles, amphibians, and fish are vertebrates.

"warm-blooded" An outdated term for animals such as today's mammals and birds. Their body temperature stays about the same, because they generate heat inside their bodies from the food they eat.

Index

Credits

KEY

t=top; l=left; r=right; tl=top left; tcl=top center left; tc=top center; tcr=top center right; tr=top right; cl=center left; c=center; cr=center right; b=bottom; bl=bottom left; bcl=bottom center left; bc=bottom center; bcr=bottom center right; br=bottom right

AUS = Auscape International; BCC = Bruce Coleman Collection; CBT = Corbis; GI = Getty Images; NHM = Natural History Museum, London; PD = Photodisc; PL = photolibrary.com; SH = Shutterstock; TSA = Tom Stack & Associates; WP = Wave Productions

Front cover James McKinnon
Spine James McKinnon
Back cover t David Kirshner, c Frank Knight, b James McKinnon
Endpapers Juliana Titin

PHOTOGRAPHS
13tr CBT **14**bc CBT, bcl NHM, bl TSA **17**c GI **19**tr SH **21**trc PL **24**bl and cl PL, l CBT **26**c GI **29**tcl AUS **30**bcl and r PL **40**tc SH **42**tl NHM **44**cr CBT **47**br, tl PL **48**l CBT **49**bcr and br CBT **50**b NHM **51**lc PL **52**c NHM **53**t CBT **56**tcr AUS **57**t CBT **59**br CBT **70**bl PD, l CBT **75**b Australian Museum, t GI **76**bc, br, tr, and tcr NHM, bl and tl AUS, cl and cr CBT, ct TSA **77**tl AUS **78**b CBT, c Hammer & Hammer Paleotek, tl PL **79**tc and bc PL, t and b CBT, c OLM **80**c CBT, l NHM, tr The Granger Collection **81**c and tr CBT, l PL **82**cl and cr NHM, r AUS, tcl Dinosaur National Museum **83**c WP, tr NHM **84**bl CBT **85**bc NHM, br WP **96**l CBT **164**br CBT **174**b Volker Steger/Science Photo Library **182**b CBT, t Smithsonian Institution (Chip Clark) **183**b Musée Natioinal d'Histoire Naturelle, t NHM

MAPS
Map Illustrations/Andrew Davies

ILLUSTRATIONS
Anne Bowman 75c; **John Bull** 28–29b; **Peter Bull Art Studio** 65tl, 180tcr, 180cl, 180c, 180tr, 180br; **Leonello Calvetti** 40bl, 41r, 47tr, 63tr, 87t, 178tr, bl; © **Karen Carr** 12–13b, 16–17b, 18–19b, 20–21b, 22bl, 26b, 30l, 31bcl, 40l, 40bcr, 56bl, 56l, 63tl, 63bl; **Barry Croucher/The Art Agency** 27c, 30c, 70br; **Wendy de Paauw** 86–87b; **Simone End** 19tcr, 24tc, 35r, 39tl, 42–43b, 51tc, 51br, 54bl, 55tr; **Christer Eriksson** 26tr, 31l, 31b, 45c, 60–61, 64c, 167, 174r; **Cecilia Fitzsimons/The Art Agency** 66t, 68l, 70bcr, 99br, 108tr, 108c, 112bc, 115c, 130c, 132c, 141cr, 141tcl, 144cl, 164bl; **Chris Forsey** 12c, 13c; **John Francis/Bernard Thornton Artists UK** 44l, 113c; **Murray Frederick** 77; **Lee Gibbons** 28c, 29bc, 30cl; **Malcolm Godwin** 56c; **Gino Hasler** 27bcl, 92bl; **Philip Hood/The Art Agency** 95b, 99b, 104t, 106t, 106b, 108b, 114b, 120t, 140t, 141b, 179t; **Robert Hynes** 23c, 101b, 108t, 112b, 115t, 115b, 122t, 130t, 131b, 136t, 139t, 143b, 157; **Steve Kirk/The Art Agency** 30br, 68c, 92l, 97b, 103t, 104b, 105t, 109t, 109b, 116tc, 118t, 130b, 132b, 141t, 164t; **David Kirshner** 22brc, 36c, 39tr, 46–47c, 50bcl, 51c, 52bl, 53c, 54c, 65bl, 67tr, 84bc, 85c, 113tl, 126–127b, 133c, 137b; **Frank Knight** 14bl, 25tr, 27l, 42–43b, 48tr, 48–49c, 68bcl, 75r, 104tc, 109tl, 111tl, 116tcr, 120cl, 170b; **David McAllister** 72–73c; **James McKinnon** 1, 2–3, 4–5, 10–11, 16–17c, 17tcr, 18–19c, 24r, 26r, 32–33c, 34tcr, 36bl, 37b, 37t, 37tr, 40lc, 40c, 41l, 41br, 44tr, 52bc, 58–59c, 60l, 62c, 63r, 64bl, 65c, 66–67c, 71c, 68bl, 69c, 74c, 86, 88–89, 90t, 90b, 91t, 93c, 94t, 94b, 95t, 97t, 98c, 100t, 102t, 102b, 103b, 110c, 112t, 114t, 116b, 117t, 117b, 118b, 119t, 119b, 120b, 121t, 122b, 123t, 123b, 124c, 126t, 127t, 128t, 128b, 129c, 131tl, 132tr, 133tl, 133tc, 134c, 135t, 135b, 136b, 137t, 138b, 139b, 140b, 142c, 143t, 145t, 145b, 156, 171, 175, 176, 177, 178b, 179b, 180tl, 181c; **James McKinnon and Peter Bull Art Studio** 20–21b; **Colin Newman/Bernard Thornton Artists UK** 15c, 24c, 24–25b, 139tc; **Nicola Oram** 17tr, 19tc, 21tr; **Pixelshack** 41bl, 50bl, 59t, 96tcr; **Mick Posen/The Art Agency** 29tr; **Tony Pyrzakowski** 84br; **Luis Rey/The Art Agency** 45b, 53tr, 67tl, 70tr, 96b, 99t, 100b, 101c, 105b, 107c, 111c, 121b, 138t, 144t, 144b, 180cbr; **John Richards** 30bcl; **Andrew Robinson/Garden Studio** 63b; **Peter Schouten** 34c, 34b, 34–35c, 38c, 39c, 42l, 42tc, 43c, 44b, 50c, 54l, 54bcl, 55c, 64tr, 65b, 68b, 101cl, 165; **Peter Scott/The Art Agency** 36l, 51t, 51tr, 56br, 57tr, 57b, 91b, 101t, 125c; **Marco Sparaciari** 83b; **Kevin Stead** 19tr, 21trc, 25tl, 80–81b; **Anne Winterbotham** 14bcr